Letting go of Ian

A faith journey through grief

D1639015

Monarch
BOOKS

Oxford, UK & Grand Rapids, Michigan, USA

Published by Monarch Books
an imprint of
Lion Hudson plc
Wilkinson House, Jordan Hill Road,
Oxford OX2 8DR, England
Email: monarch@lionhudson.com
www.lionhudson.com/monarch

ISBN 978 0 85721 538 3
e-ISBN 978 0 85721 539 0

First edition 2014

Acknowledgments (Additional text acknowledgments on p. 191)
Unless otherwise marked, Scripture quotations are from The Revised Standard
Version of the Bible copyright © 1946, 1952 and 1971 by the Division of
Christian Education of the National Council of Churches in the USA. Used
by permission. All Rights Reserved. Scripture quotations marked NRSV are
from The New Revised Standard Version of the Bible copyright © 1989 by the
Division of Christian Education of the National Council of Churches in the
USA. Used by permission. All Rights Reserved. Scripture quotations marked
NIV are taken from the Holy Bible, New International Version, copyright ©
1973, 1978, 1984 International Bible Society. Used by permission of Hodder &
Stoughton, a member of the Hodder Headline Group. All rights reserved. 'NIV'
is a trademark of International Bible Society. UK trademark number 1448790.
Scripture quotations marked NKJV are taken from the New King James Version,
copyright © 1982 by Thomas Nelson, Inc. Used by permission. All right reserved.
Scripture quotations marked KJV are taken from The Authorized (King James)
Version. Rights in the Authorized Version are vested in the Crown. Reproduced
by permission of the Crown's patentee, Cambridge University Press.
Extracts from The Book of Common Prayer, the rights in which are vested in
the Crown, are reproduced by permission of the Crown's patentee, Cambridge
University Press. Extracts from *Common Worship: Services and Prayers for the
Church of England* (Church House Publishing, 2000) is copyright © The English
Language Liturgical Consultation and is reproduced by permission of the
publisher.

A catalogue record for this book is available from the British Library

Printed and bound in the UK

In memory of Ian,
and the rich years of marriage and
ministry that we shared

Contents

Foreword

Caroline and I first met Ian in 1988, when he was Warden of Cranmer Hall at St John's College, Durham, and I was about to start training for ordination. We left Cranmer at the same time; he went off to be Bishop of Lewes, and I started as a curate in Nuneaton. We had a couple of holidays together, and Ian was invariably supportive and wise in numerous conversations about everything from leading a parish to what to do next. His friendship was a crucial part of my own development in ministry, something that was true for a huge number of ordinands and clergy in the Church of England. As the years went by we managed to find ourselves in more or less similar parts of the country, and kept in touch.

Ian and Jo went together in all that he did. Their ministry was joint: they worked very hard, and it was impossible to imagine one without the other. For those of us who knew them both, the loss of Ian was a tragedy. For Jo, it was of an entirely different order of magnitude and this wonderful book is the outcome. It is very much an Ian-and-Jo book, even to the last words being Ian's. Yet as always with Jo there is not a trace of the sentimental or maudlin. It is crisp and matter-of-fact, transparent and carefully shaped in its account of what being widowed meant, and in its careful yet penetrating narrative.

The penetration is all the more powerful because it comes not from purple prose or emotional passages, but from the narrowly and intensely observed experience of a journey. For me, two events shape the book. The first is, of course, Ian's death. The second is the earthquake in Christchurch, New Zealand, which found Jo in the cathedral escaping by the narrowest of margins as the tower crashed through the roof under which she and her cousin had been standing moments earlier. Through these two events, and in Ian's words in the last chapter, Jo reflects on what it means to come to terms with our own mortality.

All of us are touched by death, inevitably our own at the end. Most people avoid facing its reality until it bursts in on us. Ian and Jo lived with the reality of his mortality, and after his death Jo has reflected profoundly and practically on the impact and consequences. She has done so without the slightest element of cringe, and certainly without self-pity, and the degree to which the book moved me is a reflection of her skill in drawing us into the journey she is travelling and the way in which the reality of God's presence is demonstrated. Again there is no sentimentality, let alone a sense of diminishing the sense of loss.

Loss catches us by surprise in so many ways, and so does comfort. When I became Bishop of Durham, Jo and the family gave me the indefinite loan of Ian's cope, mitre, chasuble and stole, given to him at St John's College by the students, when he became a bishop. They are a stunning and unusual design by Juliet Hemingray. Every time I wear them (and by the grace of the cartoonists they have become somewhat iconic) I am surprised by the sense of missing Ian, but also by the sense of the providence and continuity of God. One wants to hear his voice and his wisdom, but also one knows that the God who called him is faithful. Loss and comfort are fellow travellers.

Through the book I was constantly surprised with Jo at the ways in which she found the presence of God catching her by surprise, whether in a trip to Taizé, or recovering from the earthquake on the west coast of New Zealand. The story of the journey reminded me of the reality that we plan our lives in straight lines across level country, yet we live them in blind corners, steep hills, dark forests and crooked paths. Strangers meet us, even strangers we have known well but whom we rediscover in fresh ways. Most of all, when we least expect it Christ is there, as comforter, guide, deliverer and saviour.

This is not only a book about bereavement, in many ways it is not even principally so. It is a call to renew our sense of purpose, of a journey with a beginning, a history and an end. It sets before us the reminder of the call, not only for clergy but for every human being, to be a pilgrim, a companion, a purposeful traveller to an assured home.

Justin Welby

Setting Out

It is autumn 2011 and I am sitting in the conservatory of our home in County Durham, looking down Weardale at the view that Ian loved, and setting out to reflect on the journey of the last four years, to draw together some of the threads of the unexpected pilgrimage that Ian and I found ourselves walking together.

I'm a Questioning Pilgrim

"Bishop in cancer scare" – a newspaper hoarding in Peterborough's Cathedral Square highlights one of the realities of public life, that if you are a diocesan bishop you cannot have a private illness. Clergy life, by its very nature, is public to some extent, and episcopal life is even more exposed, so that there is a fine balance to be found in seeking to be "private in the public arena". Indeed this is a problem faced by so many people who, to a greater or lesser extent, have a public aspect to their life, be they teachers, doctors, lawyers, politicians, media celebrities, or the like. It was something I had lived with all my married life.

Ian had been Bishop of Peterborough for eleven years, and we had become embedded in the diocese and the three counties that it encompassed. Now we were facing serious illness and an uncertain future, with implications that might be not just physical, but also emotional, mental, and spiritual – implications that might have an impact on family, work, and home; and thus the two parts of our world, the two levels on which we lived, were about to collide. We were embarking on a journey where our private experience would inevitably have to be shared in the public arena, a journey through terminal illness, bereavement, and beyond.

This is a journey faced by so many at some time in their lives, and is a familiar story, but through it run various persistent and important questions, because when God intervenes dramatically in our lives we often find ourselves being challenged to answer some of the most basic questions in life, both for ourselves and for people around us. These are the "Oh God!" questions; the "why?", "what?", "how?", "when?" questions.

So I want to begin the story of this journey, this "pilgrimage" story, by suggesting that it may be worthwhile to pause and outline some of those specific and inevitable questions which underlie it as the story unfolds. (Or, dear reader, you may prefer to skip through this "preface" and return to it later!)

Why does God allow those moments when life changes totally? Oh God, why? For me, in the course of a four-year span, God would intervene dramatically three times with memorably life-changing moments: first, the medical diagnosis that we all dread; then the bereavement that pulls the rug from under your feet; and then an unexpected near-death experience. They would be "determining moments" with a before and after, and each prompting the agonised question, "Oh God, why?" Each of us has these "determining moments" in our lives when something happens, or we make a decision, take a specific action, or in some way the course of our life is changed radically. They are milestones on our life's journey, milestones, perhaps, in our faith journey. Sometimes and rarely, as for me, they come in a rush, all at once, and leave us rather breathlessly trying to catch up with the new landscape and the new horizons around us.

Does having a high public profile make a difference? Ian, like most bishops, was involved in a wide range of commitments, both locally and nationally, so that General Synod, Church Commissioners, Council for Christian Unity, St John's College in the University of Durham, the House of Lords, and other bodies, all featured in his diary along with diocesan groups and committees, local civic events, and the daily pastoral work of caring for his clergy and people. Every area of this life would be affected. But how?

Does being in a faith-based job make a difference? Clergy are by definition people of faith, and they are called to serve and to live out that Christian faith in their daily life and work. Now Ian and I were facing one of the biggest challenges to that faith – the mystery of life and death. How would, could, and should, Ian bring this into his vocation and public ministry? What would be the expectations of other people and how would we relate to them? What about doubt and darkness of the soul?

What do we mean by "healing"? The other big challenge to faith that Ian and I faced was to understand what God's healing might mean in practice. We believe in a God who has power to heal and to save, a God who can work miracles. So should we look and pray for the simple solution of a miracle that would take all traces of the tumour away? Or would healing encompass body, mind, and spirit in a more holistic way? How would God answer our prayers? Would we have to learn to pray and trust God day by day, symptom by symptom? How would the church around us share in this process of seeking wholeness from God?

What about the impact on the family? It was not only Ian and I who had to face this challenge, but also our children, and the wider network of family members. The impact on each person and their reaction would be different so that there would be both a sense of "togetherness" and yet also of "individuality". And as the journey continued, the individual perceptions and experience of it would begin to vary and diverge – so how do you care for the differing needs of spouse, child, sibling, and others?

How can you be private in the public arena? Demonstrating emotion was not something that came easily to Ian and me, both being identified as "introverts" when we did the inevitable Myers–Briggs personality analysis; our natural mode was restraint. But there are always moments in life when we have to expose our vulnerability, let down our defences, and share our deepest emotions with others. We would need God's grace to know when it was right to do this publicly, when to be not just "the bishop and his wife", but fellow Christians on the journey of life.

What is my life all about now? This is the "what next?" question – the need to make sense of a changed landscape on life's journey and find a new path. When Elijah is in the wilderness escaping from the wrath of Jezebel, God asks him, not once but twice, "What are you doing here, Elijah?"

(1 Kings 19:9, 13, NRSV) and as one looks at that story, God's question raises other questions: "Where have you come from?"; "Where are you going?"; "What are you learning along the way?" In the same way, both Ian and I needed at different stages to discern God's purposes for us.

So many questions, and so many unknowns to be explored. As so often in life, answers would really only appear through experience as our story unfolded. Ian and I were pilgrims, journeying in faith. And over a short period of about four years so much happened, and the pace of life did not slacken. There was laughter and grief, joy and sorrow, moments of the totally unexpected and even bizarre, and God-given touches of glory. Keeping up with God and with the twists and turns of the journey was sometimes challenging and R. S. Thomas's words from his poem "Pilgrimages" came to mind: "He is such a fast God, always before us, and leaving as we arrive."[1]

Journeys are a wonderful metaphor for life as we look at its ups and down, its twists and turns, its joys and disappointments. If we are wise we take time to enjoy the landscape around us, to notice the details, to listen, and to learn. If we are lucky we may share the journey with congenial and interesting companions, or meet people along the way, and there may also be times when travelling alone may be a preference or a necessity. If we are sensible we know we will require sufficient stamina for the journey and appropriate resources, but often these may be limited and we may have to know that enough is enough. Journeys vary in length and the goal may be clear or obscured, the route well-trodden or new territory. And there is also a sense in which each person's appreciation of a journey is individual and personal – there are things that only they have seen, heard, felt, and experienced on the way, and rather like a witness in a court of law, their perception of details may vary from that of fellow travellers.

Ian and I embarked on our journey together, onto an unfamiliar path, aware of the final end, but without guidance or route map to show the way; a journey to be shared with family, friends, and colleagues; with the diocese, the church and the wider world; with strangers as well as intimates. This journey would be a balancing act: a private pilgrimage shared with many travelling companions, and yet a public pilgrimage which hid a private grief. John O'Donohue, in his book of blessings entitled *Benedictus*, writes that "a journey can become a sacred thing",[2] and when a journey takes on the attributes of a pilgrimage we find deeper, spiritual significance, especially as we look towards a destination that may or may not have been chosen, and may or may not be welcome.

When you travel, you find yourself
Alone in a different way,
More attentive now
To the self you bring along,
Your more subtle eye watching
You abroad; and how what meets you
Touches that part of the heart
That lies low at home…

When you travel,
A new silence
Goes with you,
And if you listen,
You will hear
What your heart would
Love to say.

A journey can become a sacred thing…

May you travel in an awakened way,
Gathered wisely into your inner ground;
That you may not waste the invitations
Which wait along the way to transform you.

John O'Donohue[3]

Context for a Journey

Journeys, like stories, have contexts and beginnings, and we need to start by meeting the principal travellers and discovering the initial landscape. There is a popular TV programme, *Who Do You Think You Are?*, which sets out to explore the importance of our individual identity in the context of our family background, as well as some of the inherited factors and accidents of history that have, perhaps, made us the people that we are. It is part of the complicated context that feeds into our personal story, our life's journey, and can open up new insights. So, who am I?, who are we?

My parents were both New Zealanders. My mother came of an early Church Missionary Society (CMS) family, her great grandfather having arrived with his wife and two small boys in the North Island as a CMS catechist in 1833, and she had a quiet, firm, high church, Christian faith. My father was a thoroughly sceptical agnostic, and an active senior, well-respected Freemason. His family had gone to New Zealand from Northern Ireland in the 1880s to escape the Troubles and were a wonderful mixture of staunch Church of Ireland protestants and serious Plymouth Brethren. I have a fearsome photograph of a great-great-uncle who was said to be "a fine preacher" and who appears to have looked just like Rasputin! Somehow my father, a clever, debonair, ambitious, newly qualified doctor won the heart of the elegant, intelligent, beautiful daughter of the Stipendiary Magistrate in Wanganui. Aspiring surgeons had to do their FRCS qualification in the UK; my mother's uncle was already a consultant and professor at University College Hospital in London, and so it was that my parents were married in England and, after a brief return to New Zealand, finally settled here in 1930s.

I grew up going to Sunday school at my local Church of England church and being sent to a Woodard boarding school thus receiving a good grounding in high church Anglicanism. My mother had a way of quietly winning discussions over major decisions. At university I encountered a Christian Union mission in my first year and an evangelical challenge to my rather formal Christianity; now my faith moved from my head to my heart. I joined a small Christian choir, the Ichthyan Singers, and I met Ian who came from a strong evangelical Christian family whose roots included links back to Henry Martyn, the late eighteenth-century missionary who was much revered by my CMS great-great-grandparents.

Both Ian's parents were mathematicians and teachers, and his grounding in faith and biblical knowledge came from his childhood, as did his love of the natural world and the simple joys of being out in the countryside and walking the hills. One of my early introductory visits to his home was memorable for strawberries fresh from the garden, country dancing on the lawn, and learning to canoe! Besides an inherited ability for music and maths, and a love of poetry, he had an adventurous curiosity in all things natural or mechanical – he learned to fly with an RAF scholarship while at school, his first car was a 1933 Morris Ten Four – a family hand-me-down with character – and he loved DIY in all contexts.

At the end of a term in my second year at university I drove home to London with Ian who was en route to his family in Sherborne. We arrived at lunchtime to find that my mother was out, and only my father was there to make polite conversation to this young undergraduate accompanying, and possibly attached to, his daughter. The obvious question was "What are you reading at university?" Ian's reply, "theology", was received with a short stunned silence and then "Good God!" Later in the afternoon I received the robust paternal advice about not marrying a clergyman however charming he was.

The rest, of course, is history. My father came to adore and respect Ian, though never apparently moving in his own convictions. He was even heard to defend the virtues of an ordained son-in-law to a wealthy city friend of his who was faced with a similar problem. The reluctant father getting no support from my father, and whose objections probably focused more on the financial than the philosophical, then appealed to my mother for sympathy and advice asking,

"What would the young couple live on?" He received the response, "On faith, hope, and father."

A graduate in maths and theology, Ian was thwarted in his plans to spend a year or so teaching at a Bible college in India and instead went from university to ordination training in Bristol. The timing seems incredible now, but Ian's bishop insisted on marriage taking place either before or after the diaconate year but not during it, so being impatient we opted for "before" and were married just two weeks before Ian was ordained deacon, and he went straight from honeymoon to retreat! At that stage I was still a solicitor's articled clerk and did my finals and qualified in the ensuing year. That we survived all of this is a reflection on the blind enthusiasm and optimism of youth.

Our first twelve years were spent in London, first in a curacy in south London, then on the staff at Oak Hill Theological College in north London, and then back south of the river to Mortlake where Ian was rector of a team ministry. Then in 1983, with our three children, Robert, Paul, and Elizabeth, we moved to the north-east – unknown territory for us – and we went to St John's College, Durham, where Ian became Warden of Cranmer Hall, the theological part of the college, and nine very happy years ensued.

The next move was into the episcopate; Ian was consecrated in Westminster Abbey in 1992 and became suffragan Bishop of Lewes in the diocese of Chichester. After a brief four years in East Sussex he was appointed Bishop of Peterborough and we moved into the Bishop's Lodging. This formed part of the old Bishop's Palace in the Minster

Precincts, which sounds deceptively grand but came with history and draughts in almost equal measure, being a wonderful building going back to monastic times in the thirteenth century, but adapted by every generation since to be both a home and also offices for the bishop and for the diocese. So it was large and a challenge to heat, a hive of activity and a hub for the diocese despite being located at one extreme end of it. Indeed one nineteenth-century Bishop of Peterborough once commented: "My diocese is shaped like a pear and I live on the end of the stalk."[4] However, it was a home that we loved because it offered space that could be shared: space for entertaining; space to welcome clergy and laity from the diocese; space for family and friends.

By 2007, Ian was sixty-two years old and we were in our eleventh year in the diocese. Retirement was merely a distant prospect, and Ian was still in the full flow of a rewarding and enjoyable ministry. I had retired a year before from part-time practice as a probate solicitor, but was involved with the NHS as a Non-Executive Director on the local Primary Care Trust (PCT). We still had our lovely holiday house at Lanehead at the top of Weardale, bought during our time at Cranmer Hall, and a small terrace house in Durham which would eventually become our geriatric pied-à-terre, and in a moment of madness when property in France and the euro were both cheap we had bought a small town house at St Aignan in the Touraine to ensure the possibility of escaping to the sunshine. Life was good and full of potential.

And then...

Then the landscape changed; the context of our lives changed. Context is so important, because nothing actually happens in isolation, it is always part of a wider context whether we realise it or not. Our lives are lived in the context of the physical world around us: of people and relationships; of events and history; of the mundane and the spectacular. That context is part of the landscape of the journey. There is often a temptation to say "If only..." on the assumption that if circumstances had been different or if we had made different decisions then things might have turned out better. But we are the people that we are, shaped by the experience of our lives, by our virtues and our faults, and shaped by the people and the world around us. Sometimes that context is wonderful and positive; sometimes it seems as though everything is conspiring against us. This is the rough and the smooth of the journey, the steep path, the muddy field, the sandy seashore, the grassy field. But it is the given in which we find ourselves, and where we will encounter the next stage of the journey.

The year 2007 was one of those years when everything seemed to be out of kilter – not just for us but also on the wider horizon. It was a year when it rained all summer and there was widespread flooding across England; the year when Northern Rock failed and the reality of a growing economic crisis became apparent; the year when the Anglican Communion was preparing for the Lambeth Conference amid tension and potential boycotts. On a personal level, it was one of those years when if things could go wrong then they did, and if the bizarre could happen then it did.

There were times when we didn't know whether to laugh or cry. We went to open-air Shakespeare, and saw Julius Caesar die in a puddle, and the lovers' woodland tryst in *A Midsummer Night's Dream* become an equally soggy affair. We were invited to the opera at Garsington and as the rain cascaded off the canvas roof the chorus in *La Donna del Lago* sang about "torrents of water flowing down". We holidayed in France and sat on the terrace twice and picnicked once, and at Lanehead we wore fleeces, filled hot water bottles, and lit fires. Robert and I, together with his partner Susan, achieved a five-hour walk up Cross Fell in the Pennines, but despite a good weather forecast it turned out to be cold, windy, damp, and boggy, and for two hours we were in cloud, and only able to find the summit by compass-bearing.

Then there were changes and challenges in the "day job" at The Palace. Ian's wonderfully capable secretary had decided that, after ten years, it was time to move on to new pastures and new challenges and we knew that we would miss her both professionally and as a friend. Meanwhile the Church Commissioners were planning for builders to move in and disrupt life in order to create much needed new office space, and, while daunting, this was also an exciting project because it would open up and restore an area of The Palace known in Tudor times as "Heaven's Gate", but much altered and "mangled" in the intervening centuries.

Fortunately the children's lives had a greater degree of normality and positive excitement. Liz had acquired a teaching job, a flat, and a car; Robert and Susan were celebrating a successful operation on a long-term ankle problem of Susan's by booking the holiday of a lifetime to Peru to climb to Machu Picchu along the Inca trail; and Paul was planning to go globe trotting to New Zealand to visit a friend. But as we looked around our family and friends we felt that we were counting more "downs" than "ups", with a lengthening list of people with a variety of needs and crises including accident, illness, bereavement, job prospects, etc. These were folk whom we were supporting with tea, coffee, a listening ear, TLC, and prayer, as appropriate.

It was a busy and eventful context, and in addition there was the usual busy episcopal summer with ordinations, meeting of the House of Bishops, General Synod in York, the Methodist Conference, the St Peter's Day celebrations for the cathedral and diocese, and so on – and Ian was not feeling well. He had a persistent cough, and from May onwards of that year he began to lack energy and enthusiasm and was having problems with his voice, which is not helpful for a bishop. We thought in terms of post-viral fatigue syndrome (PVFS) and began to wonder if a planned trip to our link diocese in Kenya in September would be sensible for us. Everyone told us that he needed a good holiday, but by the end of August we had tried that remedy both in France and in Weardale and Ian was getting worse, not better!

So at the beginning of September he went onto "light duties", we withdrew from the trip to Kenya, and the round of diagnostic investigations began. And so a mystery illness became a matter of public concern and prayer in the diocese, because people tend to feel an ownership of "their" bishop and to take note of his every cough or sneeze. It was no longer a private matter, nor was there going to be a quick solution, and we would have to field patiently a great many solicitous enquiries in the ensuing weeks. Indeed as the medical world engaged in their detective work, we realised that this clearly was going to be a classic plot worthy of Miss Marple or Poirot, where we, and the diocese, would have to wait for the final denouement on the last page without knowing how many chapters there were. Meantime there was an unexpected sub-plot concerning our son Paul who was diagnosed with diabetes just before his departure to New Zealand. His trip went ahead but with emergency medication and fierce instructions for a healthy regime and diet! So what next?

Waiting was not easy – it never is, though it is often necessary. But Ian and I, in our different ways, had to learn to tune in to what God wanted to say to us, to listen, to try to understand, and to become aware of the many ways in which God's word could penetrate our consciousness. For me in that limbo time it was one of the regular "Word for the Week" emails circulated by the Lawyers' Christian Fellowship each Monday that brought God's word. The spiritual focus for the first week in September of 2007 was from the prophet Habakkuk: "I will stand my watch and set myself on the rampart, and watch to see what He will say to me… though it linger, wait for it; it will certainly come", and the comment on that passage was: "Waiting can be hard. We want answers now! We can be baffled by God's delays, but God sends his answers in his own good time. We must learn to rest patiently, knowing that God will give us answers and that his timing is always perfect."[5]

And we waited through September, through October, through frustrating inactivity, through visits to doctors, clinics and hospital, through multitudes of tests and the time needed to process results. We waited with both hope and fear in our hearts, and with growing apprehension. We waited for an answer. God's answer.

Moments of great calm
kneeling before an altar
of wood in a stone church.
In summer, waiting for the God
to speak; the air a staircase
for silence; the sun's light
ringing me, as though I acted
a great role. And the audiences
still; all that close throng
of spirits, waiting, as I,
for the message.
Prompt me, God;
but not yet. When I speak,
though it be you who speak
through me, something is lost.
The meaning is in the waiting.

R. S. Thomas[6]

Part One

A "determining moment". It is 25 October 2007. We are sitting in a consulting room in Harley Street and a gentle professional voice is saying, "I have the results of the biopsy. It confirms mesothelioma. I am so sorry." And then he leaves us alone for a few moments and we hold hands and try to absorb the enormity of what he has just said.

God of the Unexpected

The waiting was over. In terms of modern medical practice it had been relatively short. Ian had had the advantage of referral to the consultant physician who looks after the bishops and had had expedited investigations including eventually three days in the London Chest Hospital for a thoracoscopy, an invasive and unpleasant diagnostic procedure. Somewhere along the line the question had been asked as to whether Ian had ever had exposure to asbestos (difficult to determine when the time span needs to be measured in decades!). A brief session on the internet had revealed the range of serious potential consequences, including cancer, that could result from particles of asbestos which had been absorbed years earlier and lingered unobtrusively in the body. Now our worst fears had been confirmed. We had an answer and our lives were about to take a wholly unexpected direction.

The stoical optimism of the last few weeks and months had suddenly been dealt a hefty blow. Earlier in the year I had written to friends that "healthy active people like us fill our lives and our diaries to excess and do not reckon on the inconvenient interruption of ill health beyond coughs and colds", and so during that long summer it had taken an effort of honest appraisal and acceptance to recognise that Ian was not just "below par" and "tired" but, perhaps, seriously unwell, and, perhaps, suffering from post-viral fatigue syndrome (PVFS).

But now, after an autumn of tests, we had to face the fact that it was not something relatively simple (and fashionable!) like PVFS, but pleural mesothelioma, a cancer of the lung cavity, treatable but not curable, and with a poor prognosis. We had googled mesothelioma and we knew some of the facts in our heads, but nothing had quite prepared me. I knew that it was uncommon and incurable, and that the timeline was variable and not very long. "How long?" I asked the hospital registrar. There was no finesse in his answer and no gentle let down – "Probably nine months to a year," he said.

"No one expects the Spanish Inquisition!" – this is one of those irritating quotations from *Monty Python's Flying Circus* that one's children tend to produce on random occasions. But in reality life is full of the unexpected and each of us has to find out how to cope with it and to learn from it. Ian and I had expected that we would have an active and enjoyable retirement together after a wonderfully fulfilling ministry in Peterborough – not that Ian would develop a rare and incurable cancer while still busily in office as a bishop. But our God is a God of the unexpected, and asks us to trust him, and to discover his love and care for us in the most unlikely circumstances. We were embarking on a new journey, with a fixed destination but no clear route map or timetable. It would produce numerous unexpected twists and turns, with a curious balance between certainty and uncertainty as we travelled. In the event, that unexpected path, with all its uncertainties, would become this story – a story to be shared, a pilgrimage to learn from – as we sought to "keep the show on the road" and to balance our personal shock and distress with our continued sense of vocation and of God's calling.

But first, there were other people around us waiting to hear the answer, and we had to put our minds to the practicalities of how and when to share the diagnosis. It would be a week before we could see the oncologist and have a proper discussion about prognosis and future treatment options. Our priority was the family. Our daughter, Liz, was now living and teaching in Peterborough, and Paul was a frequent visitor although based in London. Robert and Susan, however, were in Peru climbing Machu Picchu so we had to give evasive replies to their email enquiries and wait a week until they returned before we could all gather together as a family to support each other and come to terms with the practical, mental, emotional, and spiritual implications of this diagnosis.

Meantime, at the Sunday Eucharist in the cathedral, a kindly retired canon asked anxiously if Ian had any more news after his hospital visit, and suddenly our courage evaporated and we could not think of what to say; we could not be convincingly non-committal and we could not, at that stage, tell him the truth and the turmoil in our hearts and minds. Liz helped us to beat a hasty retreat to The Palace, and in the privacy of our kitchen the full flood of emotion overcame us, and Ian and I both cried.

We had begun to discover that being ill is a complicated business for a public figure, and that sharing the news with wider circles of people would require careful thought and planning. In that first week Ian sent confidential emails to Archbishop Rowan, the Church Commissioners, and to his senior staff. Then, when we had greater clarity about the prognosis, it was important for him to draft a letter to all the clergy and lay ministers in the diocese, to all key civic people, and to draft a press release. I had the job of dealing with a circular letter to our friends and family.

With extraordinary timing all this activity coincided with our children's plans for a residential firework party at The Palace for Guy Fawkes weekend – God really does have a sense of humour. So the young people descended, and we had our usual bonfire and firework party for them and our local friends and neighbours, and they all enjoyed themselves, oblivious to the bombshell about to be released. On the Sunday afternoon they all departed and we sat down to stuff envelopes, about 800 of them, because Ian was clear that this was not something to do by email but it needed proper letters individually signed by him. Then Ian phoned his brothers, and I phoned mine. The stage was set, letters round the diocese would arrive on Tuesday, and the press release was embargoed until Wednesday, so by mid-week we would have "gone public".

That Wednesday, with the news now in the public domain, I had to attend a public Board meeting for the Primary Care Trust. I had alerted the Chief Executive and the Chairman and some of my fellow Non-Executive Directors, but it still took all my courage and self-control to cope with the ensuing four hours of discussion of NHS policy and finance, and with the expressions of sympathy. On my way there I passed the local newspaper hoarding stating baldly "Bishop in Cancer Scare", and thought, "If only it was just a scare."

Media coverage goes with the territory for a bishop and over many years we had learned to accept this, and often to welcome it. Usually of course the stories covered public occasions and public news stories, but now a private illness had become a matter for public concern. Ian's chaplain-cum-administrator was also an experienced press officer, and he was able to guide us through the wording of press releases, arrangements for press interviews, and ways of keeping the diocese informed. Inevitably the announcement of the diagnosis became a top feature in local news bulletins on radio and TV, and this prompted many responses from complete strangers across the east of England who wanted to send sympathy and support, or to share their own experiences.

The diocese were shocked by the unexpected diagnosis, though it did not seem helpful for us to elaborate on both the certainties and the uncertainties of the implications and we left them to do their own detailed research! Many felt sure that recovery or lengthy remission would be possible and perhaps this was better because it allowed us all to continue to live and work in as normal a way as possible. Ian remained a bishop, a pastor, a "father in God", and our multi-faceted lives continued. The "glass half-full" option was definitely better. And the deluge of cards, letters, and flowers was truly humbling.

Living with uncertainty is a real challenge. It involves holding the tension of remaining both realistic and optimistic, of balancing one's hopes and fears, of finding that faith can be stretched but not broken, of finding that in an incomprehensible way God has not actually let go of us. What we did feel certain about was that God was calling us to work this out in the context in which he had placed us, in the richness and fullness of our existing lives, allowing the public and the private to interact. The option of retiring at this stage did not appeal to Ian whose priority was rather the challenge of reinterpreting his vocation and faith in the light of this wholly new situation. There was however an incentive to prioritise the diary, to delegate some things, and to focus on others that he/we really wanted to do. The commitment to the diocese, with its people and places and shared Christian journey, involved a familiarity that was in itself supportive, and a degree of normality seemed preferable to a complete change of lifestyle. And what Ian learned through the months of continued ministry would eventually be distilled into sermons, magazine articles, and other resources that he shared with the diocese.

God's "word" to me on living with uncertainty came again via the Lawyers' Christian Fellowship's Word for the

Week, an inspired choice of verse and comment by one of my legal colleagues: "Hebrews 11:8: 'By faith Abraham, when called to go to a place he would later receive as his inheritance, obeyed and went, even though he did not know where he was going.' – Do you wonder sometimes where you are going, where you will be in the next few weeks, or in five, ten or fifteen years' time? Do you wonder what you will be doing then? Does that uncertainty trouble you? I confess I sometimes wish that God would send me even just a postcard with some pointers... It does not matter that we do not know the precise detail of where we are to be and what we are to do; our security should derive from our faith in a God who is faithful to his glorious promises and our lives should be given to obeying his word."[7]

But decisions needed to be made. We had discussed palliative treatment options with the oncologist, rejected radical surgery, and Ian had opted for a course of chemotherapy with a new drug which hopefully might be particularly effective since the cancer had been diagnosed in its very early stages. The problem, as ever, was the diary. Bishop's diaries are always full and juggling them for minor changes is difficult enough, but juggling them for a four-month course of three-weekly chemo is a nightmare. And then there were the non-negotiable priorities. We had planned a senior staff Advent retreat to Rome to be based for five days at the Anglican Centre, wonderfully located in the Palazzo Doria Pamphilj, and then there was the institution of Justin Welby, a former student and special friend, as a cathedral dean. And of course Christmas was coming and we wanted Ian to be well enough to participate as fully as possible in the services and the celebration. So the start of the chemo course was fixed for the week before Christmas with an interim blood transfusion to boost the energy levels.

It was a very special celebration of Christmas, inevitably emotional, but with memorable highs as well as lows. Ian presided at Midnight Communion without any problems and then recovered with an unusually lazy Christmas Day, cancelling his normal visit to one of our local prisons, but receiving a wonderful card from the prisoners who had expected to welcome him to a Christmas celebration in the prison chapel. On Boxing Day we had an invasion of members of the wider family: brothers, nephews, nieces, and others, who were instructed to come on the basis of, "Do come, do bring food, do not bring infection!"

New Year arrived with a snowy visit to Lanehead. Indeed there was lots of snow, and with clear skies and a full moon it was quite magical at night. We were almost snowed in, but the farmer's wife decided to dig us out before we could explain to her the attraction of not being able to go south again. So we returned to the next round of chemo, and to the disruption of the builders working on the new office accommodation. They were a happy and efficient crew, and in the ancient structure of The Palace their work produced several wonderful historical architectural discoveries and added another strand to the complex pattern of our life.

We had weathered the initial shock. We had absorbed the unexpected, and, in a sense, we were settling in for the long haul. And now, the totally unexpected happened again. Robert and Susan, a couple hitherto resistant to the allure of children, announced that they were going to present us with our first grandchild in September. Machu Picchu clearly had a lot to answer for! Robert had been very insistent that we should stop off for supper on our way north to Lanehead after Christmas, and somehow, with a little bit of the fabled Irish "second sight" inherited from my mother, I knew deep down what he wanted to tell us. I felt very emotional about it because Robert had been the first grandchild in my family and my mother had died just five months before he was born. This time I felt confident that Ian would live long enough to see this child and to enjoy the first few months of its early life. God was certainly not going to let the grass grow under our feet, and a busy and eventful year lay ahead.

Meantime, we had to negotiate Lent, Holy Week, and Easter. Despite being mid-chemo Ian managed to attend all the diocesan Lent Course Sunday meetings and to give the opening address. It was good to be out and about in the diocese and to appear in public even if we did have to leave early and avoid too much personal contact because of the risk of infection. And it reassured the parishes, the clergy, and people that there was a degree of normality in their bishop's life.

Holy Week and Easter were a special and profound experience for both of us. Several people had suggested and offered specific prayer and anointing for healing, but Ian had felt that this needed to be in the right context and at the right time. And so it was that at the Chrism service on Maundy Thursday, surrounded by his clergy, Ian was anointed with the newly blessed oil of healing. He then preached simply and personally, reflecting on a comment made to him by a lifelong friend with whom he had shared his diagnosis that he needed to "make friends with his mortality". He spoke of how those reflections had made him more aware of the affection he had for the world, more aware of his own limitations, and had given him a greater sense of the particularity of his God-given vocation. It was profoundly moving for everyone present – indeed you could have heard a pin drop. Then on Easter Saturday the Vigil and Confirmation service seemed such a contrast to the Christmas Midnight service because this time there was a real sense that Ian was in charge, presiding with confidence, peace, and above all, stature, and once again preaching with devastating honesty.

And so in the "realism versus optimism stakes" we entered the summer with optimism in the ascendant, trying to pace ourselves and the diary through the months ahead. The summer would make a lot of demands on our time and energy with numerous events, including St Peter's Day when the cathedral celebrated its patronal festival and the bishop traditionally had a garden party for about 1,200 people; ordinations, which were always a high point in the year when ordinands were invited to use the Palace garden for picnic parties; General Synod at York; the Methodist Conference, which that year was at Scarborough; and of course the ten-yearly Lambeth Conference which would require our being at Canterbury for nearly three weeks; and before that a week of hospitality in the diocese entertaining visiting bishops from overseas. All these events seemed to come in quick succession and Ian was going like a yo-yo between Peterborough, York, London, Scarborough, and finally, Canterbury.

There was the usual clearing of desks to be done before setting off for the Lambeth Conference, and a lot of packing and decisions like "What clothes?"; "What weather?"; "What books?"; "What creature comforts?"; and of course "What hat for the garden party at Buckingham Palace?!" Then as a minor complication, the gardener was going into hospital for a major operation and the garden was likely to have reverted to jungle by the time we came back and to be awash with fruit and vegetables! And as a more major complication Liz had found a house to buy and was wanting advice on mortgages and conveyancing.

Eventually we were on our way to Canterbury and looking forward to the stimulus of this unique international gathering. The only problem was that Ian was developing a persistent ache in his shoulder, and we hoped that it was merely the result of over-exertion in the last few weeks. And the Lambeth Conference did live up to expectation, with over two weeks of a full and varied programme both for the bishops and for the spouses. The highlights were not just the range of speakers, the big services in Canterbury Cathedral, the London Day with its Millennium March, lunch at Lambeth Palace, and garden party tea at Buckingham Palace, but the depth of sharing in bible studies, indaba groups, workshops, informal encounters over meals, in the

45

bar, or walking around the campus.

Inevitably, keeping going through the Lambeth Conference took its toll on Ian, and it was good to have private time to relax afterwards, to get away on holiday to France and to Lanehead with family, and to prepare to launch into whatever the autumn might hold. In September Ian had the next important check-up at hospital and the session proved to be unexpectedly sobering. The scan showed progression of the cancer into the diaphragm, with some areas presenting diagnostic challenge, and the shoulder problem was likely to be an enigmatic by-product. The advice was another course of chemo. There weren't really many alternatives – either Ian would go on getting more and more tired and anaemic as the cancer gradually progressed, or he had the intervention of chemo to try and arrest it again. However, the reality seemed fairly grim as the treatment was likely to be more aggressive than last time. It was also likely to drive a coach and horses through the diary, but Barts Hospital and the diocese were getting used to the tricky exercise of attempting to balance timings for treatment with episcopal priorities. It was daunting.

With God's extraordinary timing, this was also the day that our grandson was born. As we experienced the joy of becoming grandparents we had to realise that the time to enjoy it might be more limited than we had hoped. And the new course of treatment also meant that the opportunity to be a hands-on granny would be rather limited. In the event it was a week before we could manage to travel north to Leeds to see the family and the new baby, when we could combine the visit with travelling to Durham for a dinner at St John's College in Ian's honour as retiring President of Council and a newly appointed Honorary Fellow of the College.

However, the autumn's unexpected turn of events prompted serious consideration of the future and a re-think of our retirement timetable. Going on until April 2010 and Ian's sixty-fifth birthday might not be realistic. An honest appraisal of the summer made it clear that even if the treatment was successful Ian would not have the energy levels he had previously enjoyed and would be unlikely to fulfil the demands and expectations placed on a diocesan bishop. Certainly he would not be able to fulfil them to his satisfaction. So, the big decision had to be made. The Queen gave her approval, the Archbishop countersigned the Deed of Resignation, and Ian announced that he would retire the next summer at the end of July with a farewell celebration on St Peter's Day. There would be time to plan the practicalities of moving, and time for Ian to wind down and guide the diocese towards an interregnum. We felt confident that this was the right decision, and the right time to go.

But this was not going to be a quiet wind-down. Rarely, if ever, on this journey were we allowed quiet and fallow moments, but always there seemed to be another surprise around the corner. This time it was the BBC who had chosen to come to Peterborough Cathedral for the Christmas celebrations and to televise both the Midnight Communion and the Family Service on Christmas morning. It was all very exciting, all requiring a lot of preparation, organisation, and rehearsal, and so different for us from our experience of Christmas the previous year. Despite being mid-chemo Ian was able to rise to the occasion and preside with confidence at the Midnight service, disappearing at times into the clouds of incense which the BBC found so atmospheric for their camera shots. I read the Old Testament lesson, and Liz was one of the stewards, so it was a time of full family involvement for our last Christmas in the cathedral. It felt like a real celebration of faith and hope. And we were sharing this celebration publicly across the TV networks with family, friends, and strangers!

And so we entered 2009. Journeys have beginnings and ends, milestones, twists and turns, ups and downs, and we felt that perhaps 2009 might have all of those. The path was feeling gently downhill and we hoped that it would be a gentle, active, and lengthy downhill. At our New Year senior staff party we were asked to look ahead not by making new-year resolutions but by choosing just two words to take with us into the year ahead. Ian said, "still living", and I said, "travelling hopefully". Not a bad summary, really.

As Ian emerged from the second course of chemo we had to put our minds to the first part of our removal which would be all the furniture which was going to Lanehead, together with all the books that Ian wanted to take and for which he had already found time and energy during the spring to build a set of shelving in the new library. (As one does, mid-chemo!) So, in a week in March we were off (with Bishop's Move of course!), and a merry crew of removers who discovered the joys of Upper Weardale and the problems of man-handling a heavy Bluthner grand piano over rough ground from a farm track.

Before the move, while we still had not one but two grand pianos in our hall at The Palace, we had enjoyed the opportunity to entertain all the High Sheriffs and Lord Lieutenants in office during our time in the diocese to a farewell soirée with a two piano recital. In fact, there were two soirées on consecutive evenings because with the diocese covering three counties we had known thirty-nine High Sheriffs and six Lord Lieutenants (and their spouses), during our thirteen years in the diocese. It was an opportunity to enjoy, and thank, this rich range of people also in public office whom we had got to know and appreciate.

Lent brought the familiar round of diocesan Lent courses, and this time we were accompanied by Liz who was trying to recruit young people to join a group to go on pilgrimage to Taizé in France in the summer. This was something we had originally hoped that Ian would lead, but that was looking increasingly unlikely. Holy Week and Easter were again memorable times, with Ian being anointed at the Chrism service, and then presiding at the Vigil and Confirmation on Easter Eve.

We were post-chemo, optimistic, and heading for retirement in the summer. We had a post-Easter break at Lanehead when Ian unpacked his books and enjoyed playing the piano, which was now taking up an inordinate amount of space in the library. He was totally relaxed and at peace with himself in the place that he loved. As we came south I delivered him to Bishopthorpe in York for a two-day meeting of the House of Bishops, then collected him off a train in time to go out to a civic dinner at Deene Park, a house which is one of the Tudor jewels of Northamptonshire and a perfect setting for black tie elegance. Then we celebrated his sixty-fourth birthday, and had a weekend away in Wharfedale at Parcevall Hall with our bishops' cell group for reflection, prayer, sharing, and support. Then it was time for another hospital check-up.

The clinic appointment on 1 May was disappointingly and unexpectedly sobering. The oncologist and the GP were clear that Ian was likely to have at most only two or three months more, that moving was out of the question, and that we might not make it to St Peter's Day and our official farewell. Suddenly after eighteen months we were facing hard reality; we had reached the end of the beginning, and the beginning of the end. The future was no longer open-ended, and we had to find the resources, and the honesty, to face and share with each other the deep and differing range of emotions we were feeling – trusting God had never been more difficult. Meantime we had maintained our public profile, and Ian had continued to be involved in the diocese as normally as possible so that for most people there had been little concept that the sands of time were running out. Once again Ian sent emails to the Archbishop, the Church Commissioners, and his senior staff. Now it was time to prepare the diocese and the parishes for the hard truth and the rapidly shortening time span. So as we set off for a weekend in Somerset to celebrate the ruby wedding anniversary of long-standing friends, I was driving and Ian had pencil and paper to hand as we tried to word the email that he would send round to clergy and lay ministers. It was not an easy exercise and we never did complete it – God had other plans! Once again the unexpected was just round the corner!

Sing, my soul, when hope is sleeping,
Sing when faith gives way to fears;
Sing to melt the ice of sadness,
Making way for joy through tears.

Sing, my soul, when sickness lingers,
Sing to dull the sharpest pain;
Sing to set the spirit leaping;
Healing needs a glad refrain.

Sing, my soul, of him who shaped me,
Let me wander far away,
Ran with open arms to greet me,
Brought me home again to stay.

Sing, my soul, when light seems darkest,
Sing when night refuses rest,
Sing though death should mock the future:
What's to come by God is blessed.

John L. Bell and Graham Maule[8]

Being Honest with God

"Out of the depths have I cried to you... Lord, hear my voice" (Psalm 130:1–2, NKJV). Sometimes, the only thing we can do is to be honest and cry to God. For me, as a lawyer and a "word merchant" it helps to articulate my deepest thoughts and feelings by putting them on paper, where somehow they become more manageable. My private journal became an important companion in the weeks and months ahead helping me to face each new stage, each new decision; it became my way, indirectly, of talking to God. And my responses moved on with time. I found myself reflecting on the stages of shock, and on the range of reactions and emotions experienced – beginning with the feeling that the bottom had fallen out of the world, with numbness, disbelief, depression, physical aches, imagining, and thinking through the worst problems and scenarios. Then gradually getting a positive grip, finding things that can be done and planned that ease the sense of powerlessness, realising that often you are ministering to other people as they minister to you.

So I look back through my journal and can draw out some of the ways in which I learned to cope with what was happening in my life, as well as what was happening to my grasp on faith and on my relationship to God. By looking back in this way, I have found that various themes emerge to give different perspectives on the road that we were travelling, and yet together they interweave, rather like Celtic knotwork, to form a complex pattern of emotion and experience.

So back to October 2007 and that limbo week when we had diagnosis but not prognosis, and no announcement had been made. I was sitting in a café on the Edgware Road in London on my way to a singing lesson and I felt the urge to take out pen and paper and try to articulate the turmoil within me by committing my thoughts to paper: "I feel in a state of suspended reality, as though I am walking in a dream. I am curiously numb, unable to cry, not even angry, just vastly disappointed. I cannot believe that this is happening to me. It is all so disorientating, and changes my perspective on life and death, on values, on motivation. Physically there is this knot in my stomach that will not go away, the symptom of a tension and deep-seated fear and foreboding that seems to grip me. And yet I have to continue through the motions of everyday life. Prayer is difficult because it requires an honesty with myself and with God that I am not certain I can muster. I think of Dag Hammarskjöld's words 'For all that has been, thanks' and I am able to count so many blessings and good memories, but can I really pray the next part – 'For all that is to come, yes'?[9]

The reality and the details and all the complications are too vast for me to take in and give assent to."

Music brings its own solace, and in my singing lesson the words from a beautiful aria in Mendelssohn's *Elijah* brought elements of both comfort and challenge: "O rest in the Lord, wait patiently for him." Yes, I could learn from that and let the music calm my mind; but the next part: "and he shall give thee thy heart's desire", no, because my heart's desire was for this nightmare to go away! "Commit thy way unto Him, and trust in Him", well, there was no other option. Perhaps the words of a Lutheran hymn with its solemn music as set by Benjamin Britten at the beginning of *Noye's Fludde* came nearer to expressing my troubled thoughts: "Lord Jesus, think on me, nor let me go astray; through darkness and perplexity, point thou the heavenly way."[10]

There were practicalities that brought us down to earth. We were advised that we needed to put our affairs in order – we needed to review our Wills and our finances. Ian began to outline his funeral service and to discuss with the Dean a possible burial location within the cathedral precincts. And we needed to accelerate our plans for reordering Lanehead so that if possible it would move from being a holiday house to being a comfortable retirement home.

Lurking in the background was the question of whether Ian should think about bringing forward his retirement, and this raised issues on so many levels. From a practical point of view there was a lot of work to be done at Lanehead that required both time and effort. Then winding down an episcopal diary is easier said than done.

I learned how to reply to people's well-meant enquiries, "Will Ian be all right?" The honest reply was, "Yes, in the short term, but in the long term, no." The unanswerable question was to know how long the short term might be! At the end of the first course of chemo the medics were optimistic and felt that we might be able to push the boundaries towards the longer known survival times of two to three years. In some ways the greatest challenge was just the uncertainty of how the future would work out, and the need to be disciplined and focus on the "what is" rather than the "what if". In modern parlance we moved from "how long is a piece of string?" to "how long is a piece of elastic?"

Meantime I had to watch and support Ian through the first course of treatment. And chemotherapy really can be awful. You have to believe that it is going to provide some worthwhile benefit as you go through the cycle of weeks, moving from a grim first week to a more stable second week, and finally feeling fine for a week before starting all over again! I needed to be persuaded by the GP that while he was still relatively young and fit the course could result in suppression of the cancer so that Ian had a sufficient and reasonable amount of energy, both physical and mental, to live and work at a level he could accept without frustration. Later, when Ian embarked on a second course of chemo, I found it even more difficult, and the regime was more aggressive. I found myself asking God if this was how it had to be? And the reassurance came through the wonderful support and encouragement of the GP, the oncologist, and the nurses who looked after Ian.

Our times away at Lanehead were very important. There was a sense of normality when we were there, not of denial but of enjoyment of familiar life in the present moment with opportunities to relax and discuss. We talked rarely but honestly about the future, and we both appreciated that the issue was not "if" but "when". I listened to Ian talking about potential options and preferences, and I realised that my role was just to listen and to adapt my own thinking – and to pray. I needed to pray for the wisdom and the patience to walk alongside him.

Easter 2008 was a turning point for me. On Palm Sunday I was in the cathedral and Ian was at home reading W. H. Vanstone's *The Stature of Waiting* and starting to write his sermon for the Chrism service on Maundy Thursday. I thought ahead through the days of Holy Week knowing that on Thursday Ian would join his clergy for the renewal of ministerial vows and would have the opportunity to preach and share with them his reflections of this journey. He had also chosen that occasion, surrounded by his clergy, to be anointed by his suffragan bishop with the oil of healing. And now God brought home to me that we were on very different journeys. Holy Week would mark for me the beginning of Ian's separate path, and the acknowledgment that my own path was another, no less demanding, journey alongside. I had to let him go, acknowledge the individuality of our journeys, and watch. In the autumn I had let go of our dreams and hopes for the future and for our retirement, and now I had to begin to let go of Ian himself.

Letting go – ah, but that is easier said than done. I am someone who likes the status quo and resists change; someone who is by nature acquisitive and treasures both things and people, and dislikes moments of parting. To accept that I was giving up my life's companion, and my dreams, and all our hopes for the future, was really hard, and would take time – lots of time – but in a curious way it was also liberating.

The autumn of 2008 brought so many conflicting emotions. There was the joy at the birth of our grandson and the wonderful sense of fulfilment that Ian would see and hold and know his grandson. I had continued to be so conscious of the fact that my mother had died five months before Robert, her first grandchild, was born and I had found myself revisiting that very emotional period of my life, often rather tearfully. Now I could echo the prophetic words: you shall "turn their mourning into joy… and make them rejoice from their sorrow" (Jeremiah 31:13, KJV).

But on the other hand, as Ian embarked on a second course of treatment, I found that adjusting my mindset to a journey with a new pattern of plateaux and dips was easier said than done. There were just too many balls in the air, for both of us, and occasionally I just got tired of coping. Now that Ian had announced his retirement an element of panic set in as I contemplated all that would need to be done and sorted by the next summer, while keeping our other priorities and commitments going. I felt very "low key" as we entered onto a chemo cycle again, and I resented the struggle to juggle the diary yet again. My prayers must have been a depressive moan! And things were not helped by reading of the death of one of our fellow "patients" who had stayed in the "sanatorium" wing at the Lambeth Conference. David had been a cheerful optimistic South African bishop, determined to come to Lambeth despite his cancer, and thrilled to be presented to the Queen at the garden party. He had died unexpectedly of septicaemia following a course of chemo. Oh God, why?

There were times when sheer exhaustion set in. In the week before Christmas there was a performance of Handel's *Messiah* in the cathedral, and I found that I was so tired that I had to leave during the interval, go home to bed at 9 p.m., and sleep for nine hours! It was truly an occasion to echo the psalmist's words that God "gives to his beloved in sleep" (Psalm 127:2, variant RSV reading).

There were times when I found it hard to live with the indeterminate timeline, and the different scenarios that might unfold. Even more difficult was it to cope with other people's perception, or lack of perception, of the complexities that this brought to some of the decision-making for the future. Together, and publicly, we were planning a "business as usual" retirement, while privately we were conscious that there was always the "but" factor. Publicly, Ian was seen to be coping normally, but privately he was experiencing decreasing energy and increasing pain. At times living became an act of the will, not of the heart. Prayer, likewise!

Then the new clear prognosis, the knowledge that the cancer was spreading, and that the direction of the journey was now downhill, and at a fairly rapid rate, and that the journey's end was probably in sight. And I felt that, in a way, nothing had changed and yet everything had changed; there was a whole new perspective: faith, hope, love, all had new meanings. I realised that to cope I had to look outwards and upwards, not inwards. Faith was being stretched again.

We were reaching journey's end, and I felt numb and afraid, yet there was a relentless momentum that kept us going, hanging on to a degree of normality, living each day as it came. We asked friends and family to pray with us that we might "go with the flow" and accept God's timing and plans for us. For me, reliance now had to be on the support of our family and the prayers of the many people who had been travelling faithfully with us. Over to you, God!

When near the end of day, life has drained
Out of light, and it is too soon
For the mind of night to have darkened things,

No place looks like itself, loss of outline
Makes everything look strangely in-between,
Unsure of what has been, or what might come.

In this wan light, even trees seem groundless.
In a while, it will be night, but nothing
Here seems to believe the relief of dawn.

You are in this time of the interim
Where everything seems withheld.

The path you took to get here has washed out;
The way forward is still concealed from you.

The old is not old enough to have died away;
The new is still too young to be born…

What is being transfigured here is your mind
And it is difficult and slow to become new,
The more faithfully you can endure here,
The more refined your heart will become
For your arrival in the new dawn.

John O'Donohue[11]

Counting Blessings

A friend who had recently lost her husband after many years of caring for him through a degenerative illness received a letter of sympathy, which included the comment: "You must feel so angry with the God who has let you down so badly." We know each other well enough to be totally honest, and we could agree that neither of us had ever felt angry with God. But we had felt disappointed, and bewildered, asking the inevitable questions of "why?" and "what?": "God, what are you doing?"; "God, why is this happening?"; "God, what about healing?" We wished that things had worked out differently, that God had approved all the plans that we had in mind for our lives. Instead we had had to absorb the reality of God's words in Isaiah: "My thoughts are not your thoughts, neither are your ways my ways" (Isaiah 55:8). Indeed, she and I both felt that we had had to learn anew to trust God and as we journeyed we had encountered numerous unexpected blessings.

We in the West live in an age of affluent secularism,

where we like to be in control and where faith is seen as irrelevant and irrational; where belief in blind and random forces of nature is preferred to a God who may be seen as capricious, cruel, or remote – the God who can let you down. Faith has become elusive, unfashionable, neglected, and often subject to political correctness. This is the challenge for the twenty-first century Christian pilgrim. And if we are honest, we all struggle to reconcile faith and doubt, to seek for coherence and continuity in our lives, and in our world. In the epistle to the Hebrews we read that "faith is the assurance of things hoped for, the conviction of things not seen" (Hebrews 11:1) and we crave that conviction, that freedom from doubt. Faith sees the blessings that come in spite of ourselves, in spite of the "slings and arrows of outrageous fortune". It sees the seeds of hope that grow from pain and loss, it sees the sunshine through the clouds. Everyday life with its ups and downs, with its crises and challenges, is the vehicle for discovery of faith, but only if we stop and think, ask the deeper questions and reflect. Of course doubt lurks, and events occur which tempt us to question the faith that we hold, but there is more than a grain of truth in the old chorus "Count your blessings, count them one by one, and it will surprise you what the Lord has done."[12] So it is worth looking back and recounting some of the things that meant most to Ian and myself, and some of the ways that we were enabled to look at life with thankfulness, with humour, with surprise.

Our house at Lanehead offered us wonderful blessings as well as lots of hard work as we did all the necessary improvements. New Year 2008 was magical with snow and the new moon. February half-term, when the builders were busy converting and plastering the garage, re-plastering the sitting room, and creating new larder and airing cupboard spaces, produced one of those amazing weeks when the weather was warm and sunny, temperatures reached 14°C in the shade and 19°C in the sun, and we were able to open all the doors and windows and let the air flow through the house to dry out the new plaster.

Time and again the children brought their own unique blessings. There was the excitement of anticipating our first grandchild. Paul was about to embark, unexpectedly, on a serious romance. Liz was living and working in Peterborough and able to add benefits and complications to our life in equal measure, and one special memory is of the fun of the mother and daughter pamper day she chose as my Mothering Sunday present in 2008.

The Lambeth Conference brought its own unique blessings. The week of hospitality before the conference brought us a wonderful mixture of bishops and their wives from South Korea, South Africa, Kenya, Australia, and America. The two Kenyans arrived after a rather impromptu decision to break ranks with some of their colleagues and to attend and came without any episcopal robes. Finding spare robes at short notice in appropriate sizes was not easy, and on the Sunday the very tall bishop from our link diocese was processing in the cathedral in a red chimere (long episcopal gown) that still had pins in it with only half the hem actually sewn!

For Ian and myself this was our second Lambeth Conference, but since 1998 the campus at the University of Kent had been improved by providing almost entirely single en suite accommodation. This created both complaints from couples who wanted to be together and moved mattresses around to the irritation of the university authorities, and also delight from some who were experiencing privacy for the first time in their lives! However for us, and for two other couples where the bishop was attending despite suffering from cancer and its complications, it was imperative that we had shared rooms, and a special "sanatorium wing" was created for us.

Ian paced himself carefully through the Conference, avoiding early mornings and late nights but engaging as fully as possible in bible studies, indaba groups, services, and meetings, and the many opportunities to mix and meet, share and discuss, and just make friends. Lambeth provides an amazing array of input, and an amazing mixture of people from across the whole of the Anglican Communion, a spiritual and cultural experience like nothing else, with a real depth of sharing.

For me it was possible to be more fully involved at each end of the day and I enjoyed the rhythm of morning eucharist and night prayer. The "prayer place", a spiritual hub located in the Senate House in the centre of the campus, became central for me, and the simple upper room arranged for worship had as its focus a stark plain wooden cross with flowers at its base which spoke to me of the harsh realities that I knew I must face and not ignore – as well as the softening bloom of hope and of God's grace.

The two weeks on site felt like a series of pilgrimage events for me. There was a workshop where we made prayer beads and my hopes and fears became focused on this simple and beautiful aid to prayer – I was able to share its significance for me (albeit tearfully). In one of our plenary spouses sessions we shared our perspectives on health and well-being and anointed each other with oil in a simple act of prayer and shared support. We spent an afternoon on a thirteen-mile pilgrimage walk into Canterbury arriving in time for evensong. We had a trip out to the Anglican Benedictine convent at West Malling in Kent where I had often spent retreat time. It was a joy to meet the sisters in their "enclosure" and share tea and worship with them. In our bible study group we shared deeply and entered the very different worlds of bishops' wives in Sudan, in the Solomon Islands, in Fiji, and in North America, England, and Scotland.

I kept a diary which I could share with the diocese on my return and my random observations expressed the range of things that I was seeing and learning. For example:

> Conference living would not be the same without
> conference bags. We all had them, full of our
> worship books, hymn books, bible study books,
> headphones (for translations), etc. – some carried
> in the hand, some on the shoulder, and one seen
> carried African-style on the head!

***

In one of our early spouses sessions we discussed our marriages and the different cultural traditions which create and shape them – those who romantically "fell in love" sharing with those who met their husband for the first time on the day of their wedding.

***

The conference ended on a high with an exuberant sense of commitment and unity at the final plenary, and a wonderful Eucharist in the Cathedral, and after that… we boogied! We had supper and a big band and it all felt rather surreal, with African bishops swaying and dancing to Latin rhythms, and certain UK bishops displaying amazing skills and energy as they jived into the night!

Archbishop Rowan had spoken in his final sermon about the Lambeth Conference as a story that can make things happen, and I found myself thinking that in a sense Ian and I were living a story, and that perhaps it too was a story that would make things happen.

Post-Lambeth holiday time brought its own blessings. Despite a fairly constant sunshine-and-showers syndrome, both France and Weardale offered opportunities to relax and feel fairly normal, and Ian indulged his passion for clocks by buying an old Vienna Regulator in the brocante street market in St Aignan and then restoring it.

Then it was September and we were on the train on our way to London for the next important check-up at hospital when Ian's mobile phone rang. Susan had been in labour for over twenty-four hours and we were beginning to worry. But here was Robert with the lovely news that we had a grandson, weighing in at a very healthy 8lb 14oz and both mother and baby doing well. It was the day before our thirty-ninth wedding anniversary and we felt very blessed – it was the first thing that we told the oncologist! Counting blessings was important that day because the medical news was not good and the CT scan showed progression of the cancer. Back home in the evening as we reviewed the ups and downs of the day with Liz and some friends, we opened a bottle of champagne to celebrate the good things in life – to celebrate the glass half-full!

Sometimes the bizarre and the humorous were never far away. Perhaps a gift of humour is one of God's greatest gifts to us. In a curious way, as life became more serious and difficult in the winter of 2008 and through into early 2009, so the opportunities to stand back and laugh (or cry) also increased.

Christmas had its moments. First there had been the long-running saga of the new telephone system for The Palace after the completion of the new office accommodation, which was still not fit for purpose despite months of explanation and effort and endless arguments over bills. This reached crisis point in the week before Christmas when the phone company actually cut us off for three days. It is not easy to run a bishop's office and home at such a busy time of year without a phone. Ian, recovering from a chemo session, found himself making irate calls on his mobile from his convalescent bed. Then negotiations around the future of Peterborough Community Services (PCS) reached their own crisis point and I had an important Board meeting to chair at which key strategic decisions needed to be made.

Two days before Christmas there was a city-wide power failure, with all sorts of consequences including my computer crashing, but at least it meant that I could not read any more emails from the NHS about PCS. Meantime, this was the week when Liz was moving out of her flat and into her new house, with all the attendant packing up, cleaning, transportation, and any last-minute legal hitches.

The Christmas services were an oasis of beauty and the family gathered at home for all the familiar and comforting rituals. After Ian's exertions at the Midnight Service, we had the laziest ever morning on Christmas Day when he stayed at home and we watched on television the Family Service from our own cathedral. But the unexpected was never far away, and at lunchtime we noticed that the hot water tank had sprung a leak and water was spreading across the floor of the utility room next to the kitchen. By some miracle we were able to contact the plumber and arrange for him to come with his mate and drain down in the evening while we rounded the day off with cheese and port. They went away with our thanks, a bottle of wine each, and the promise that we would not be able to use the system for another ten days until they could source and fit a replacement tank! It was just as well that we planned to go to Lanehead the next day.

And finally? Oh, Liz woke me on Boxing Day at 6 a.m. with such acute stomach pain that we were off to the NHS Walk-in Centre before breakfast. Painkillers and a referral to the GP seemed to be the temporary solution until we, and she, returned from our post-Christmas break.

We needed Lanehead to work its magic again and revive and energise both Ian and me. The weather turned out to be really cold and crisp, with some spectacular hoar frosts, and temperatures dropping to –8 °C. In response we were rather too enthusiastic with the open fires and managed to set fire to the sitting room chimney – again! (And no, we didn't call the fire brigade – we had already learned alternative strategies.)

We entered 2009 with Robert and Susan settling into parenthood, Liz settling into her new house, and Paul becoming anything but settled. He was planning a trip to Australia in April to research possible jobs and to meet an ex-girlfriend whom he had not seen for fourteen years and who had been renewing old friendships the previous summer via a social networking site. Somehow we got the impression that there was more to this trip than met the eye.

Once again Lent, and then Holy Week and Easter, provided a spiritual focus. This year the Vigil and Confirmation on Easter Eve was a service which seemed in every way to reach heights of praise and wonder, and to speak with profound spiritual significance. It felt like the best Easter service we had ever had – really celebratory, with liturgy and music that flowed and inspired – and it was good to experience that immense blessing from God, to experience a sense of worship that transcended everything else. The Easter greeting was heartfelt: "The Lord is risen, he is risen indeed!"

And in that Easter week Paul returned from Australia, and told us quietly, but confidently, that Sara was the girl he should have married fourteen years ago, and he hoped that she would be coming over to England in July. Ian and I searched our memory banks to try and remember what she had looked like fourteen years ago!

We felt positive as we looked forward to the summer, to our farewell, to retirement. We felt confident that God had blessed us in so many ways and that somehow it would all work out. We thought back to our time in our link diocese in Kenya when we had learned the simple response used in their church services: "God is good, all the time. All the time, God is good" – *Mungu yu mwema*.

God moves in a mysterious way
His wonders to perform;
He plants his footsteps in the sea
And rides upon the storm.

Deep in unfathomable mines
Of never-ending skill,
He treasures up his bright designs,
And works his sovereign will.

Ye fearful saints, fresh courage take,
The clouds you so much dread,
Are big with mercy and shall break
In blessings on your head.

William Cowper[13]

*T*ravelling Companions

"*Y*ou'll never walk alone"[14] – as I look back, the months and years were full of so many people who walked alongside us, sharing this journey through illness and bereavement. Very early on when friends and family started to ask us to "keep in touch" I realised that there was the potential, through email, to gather a network of "travelling companions" who would be able to support us and pray for us on this unfamiliar journey that we were embarked upon. They may have formed a core, but the network spread much wider including, of course, our diocese with all its parishes, clergy, people, and its secular and civic life. It was at times like this that I realised what an amazing range of contacts we had gathered over the years and in so many different walks of life, one of the consequences of living a public life, and what a privilege it was.

Particular people contributed their own gifts to our unfolding story and each contribution had its place, whether great or small. There were the numerous medics, our GP, the consultant physician who pursued the diagnosis, the oncologist, the nurses in clinic and in the chemo ward; the friends who offered beds in London before clinics and treatments, and those who provided meals on wheels when we got back to Peterborough; those who sent flowers from time to time to cheer us on our way, and those who provided home-made cakes (some just left on the doorstep); those who sent the constant stream of cards and letters, and those many, known and unknown, who prayed for us.

In the millennium year of 2000 Ian had decided to do a pilgrimage walking the length of the diocese, and doing this twice, in spring and autumn, so that by following two different routes and ancient "ways" he could take in every deanery in the diocese. We had a couple of keen walkers to organise the route and together we set out on what felt like holiday rather than work. An itinerary with the route had been circulated through the diocese and each day was organised so that we started with morning prayer in one of the parish churches, lunched at another, and ended with tea and evening prayer in a third. Along the way we were joined by people who walked longer or shorter distances with us, and we made occasional stops at schools or other places en route. We had a wide range of travelling companions, and each played their part in the journey, some joining us for the long haul, some briefly for part of the walk, some being there just to provide food and drink at lunchtime, some joining us for worship at the beginning or end of the day, some providing overnight hospitality. In a similar way, we found that we had a range of travelling companions as we journeyed through Ian's terminal illness.

But the relational aspect was not always easy, raising the tricky issues of how much can be shared, and with whom, and at what level. What is helpful? What is appropriate? What do people need to know? What should remain very private and intimate? Our early experience in that limbo week when we had first received the diagnosis but not made any announcement, and when we had been unable to deal with a kindly update enquiry from one of our retired canons, had taught us something about our own vulnerability and the problem of private emotions in public contexts. Indeed that "limbo week" was important to us as a couple and as a family, because it gave us private time to give expression to the full range of our emotions, to cry together, to have big hugs, to face the reality and the shock, and to share slowly with those friends and colleagues who were very close to us. After that, we could gradually face the challenge of sharing publicly.

Our email updates were circulated every couple of months or when there was any significant development, and they served as a useful way for us to stop and review and then provide some sort of précis of progress. But progress was by no means limited to the medical; it covered all the other things that were going on in our lives and our comments on life in its widest context! We wanted our friends and family to share the fullness of this extraordinary journey, with its ups as well as its downs.

But apart from the senior staff, we did not circulate these updates to people within the diocese. Subconsciously we knew that on this more public front there was need for a degree of stability and continuity, and no need to share at a more private level. Ian was still out and about in the diocese and fully involved when he was well enough, and the reassurance of "seeing the bishop" was important. It allowed a degree of "business as usual" to continue.

And business did somehow continue as usual! Ian presided at Christmas Midnight Communion five days after his first chemo session, a bit wobbly, but fortified by steroids and supported by the comforting, larger than life, presence of our assistant bishop, John Flack, ready to take over if necessary. During the rest of the chemo programme we managed the dates so that he could give the introductory talk to each of the diocesan Lent Course meetings on Sunday afternoons around the diocese, leaving after half an hour and not mingling with folk so as to avoid any risk of infection. And regular meetings and interviews continued as ever. The warmth and encouragement experienced on these occasions made any effort worthwhile.

Some people had deeper perception, and some people's companionship occurred at specially memorable moments. Some people responded to the emailed updates with short notes of encouragement. Some came up with memorable phrases that lodged in the memory, such as the Sussex friends who reflected that we "seemed to have our theological walking boots on", and the friend (mentioned earlier) who encouraged Ian to "make friends with his mortality".

Some told me only later of their personal insights. One such was one of our parish clergy who, some two years after Ian died, told me how she still remembered that at the Diocesan Synod in the autumn of 2006 she noted that Ian had a bad cough and had remarked to him on it again at the Chrism service in Easter week in 2007 when she was surprised that it still lingered. For us it had been "just a winter ailment", but to her it had been unusual. This perceptiveness and prayerful concern were very humbling. The same woman remembered how after a special service in her church in 2005 we had discussed over lunch the problems for clergy of planning for retirement and for the unforeseen, and that I had remarked that we had recently bought our little pied-à-terre in Durham, which would be useful "if anything happened to Ian" – a throw-away remark that I forgot, but which she remembered.

Our bishops' cell group was important to us, and our annual weekend meetings occurred just after Easter each year. These were times of relaxation and of deep sharing in a context that was wholly confidential and safe, and where we were able to discuss together the balancing act for all of us between the public and private aspects of our lives. We met at Parcevall Hall in Wharfedale, a wonderful part of the Yorkshire Dales, and a place to inspire Ian to put on his walking boots and find the energy to walk and explore the countryside.

We also had a small network of prayer partners who for many years had received a print out of our weekly diary and committed themselves to pray for us. For them I would add personal comments on the back of the diary sheet outlining in more detail the ups and downs of life as each week passed. Memorably, in the last week of Ian's life, after we had shared the new prognosis and shortened timeline, one of them had sent me a postcard of a painting by Monet of fishermen hauling a boat ashore to encourage me in the remainder of the "long haul", but it proved to be amazingly prophetic since Ian's boat was indeed imminently coming ashore on the other side.

Other individuals played their part for me. The Chrism service on Maundy Thursday was always followed by a lunch at The Palace for all of the clergy, a wonderful gathering of about 150 people, and a very special focal meeting point in the year. In 2008 the clergy were still absorbing all that had taken place in the service, Ian's sermon and the anointing of him with the oil of healing, and two of the clergy individually sought me out after lunch so that they could pray with me and minister to me. That shared time was special because it helped to affirm for me both the journey that I was on with Ian, and the separate journey that I was on alone.

Journeying together with other people is a time of sharing, of both giving and taking. For us, Ian's senior staff had been very special travelling companions, sharing week by week the ups and downs of our journey, and we wanted to express our thanks to them in some tangible way. So during our post-Easter break at Lanehead in 2009 we went into Alston to our favourite potter and we had a wonderful shopping spree buying special items to give to each of Ian's colleagues as a farewell present. We spent time matching each design and colour combination to each of the individuals, and we looked forward to the final staff meeting and lunch in July when we would distribute these tokens of our love and thanks for all that they had meant to us.

Travelling companions are also people who are there when the journey ends. They can offer a degree of continuity, and I knew that for me as one journey reached its end another would begin and I would need a lot of love, help, support, and prayer to step out into that wholly new landscape.

***

Selected reflections from emailed "updates"

April 2008, after the encouraging end-of-chemo review:

> *The long term destination of this journey remains the same, this cancer doesn't go away completely; the short-term travel becomes a more interesting and more extended hike ("with our theological walking boots on" to quote one friend). There is the potential now to count in years rather than months; the oncologist talks about the importance of attitude, and we interpret that with a focus on prayer, determination, and acceptance.*

June 2008:

> *There is the underlying uncertainty, the "how long is a piece of string?" syndrome, but extended to "how long is a piece of elastic?"! Ian, inevitably, is going to be a unique patient, pushing new boundaries, and*

providing good research data – and we gently tell the oncologist not to underestimate the power of prayer and the blessings of God.

Summer 2008:

Ian's preferred option for occupational therapy is DIY with a view to more comfortable retirement options. Work on our Weardale house has progressed well and in addition to the new IKEA kitchen which we fitted at Easter, he has now laid a lovely oak floor in the garage-cum-library.

September 2008 (after the reality check at Barts Hospital):

At this point we realise that the future of this journey begins to look like becoming a series of plateaux and dips… and there's probably a hiking analogy somewhere there!

October 2008 (after the decision to take early retirement):

We are at another stage of this journey. Clearing the accumulated clutter and debris from the path – i.e. downsizing, etc. – is a challenge of immense proportions. Meantime the Pensions Board have to work out how a clergyman applying for retirement on the grounds of ill health certifies that he has told his bishop of his intention when he is the bishop! – oh, the joys of bureaucracy and box ticking.

Easter 2009 (after Ian had been anointed with oil again on Maundy Thursday):

> *By a process of "Chinese whispers" a neighbouring bishop was told the next day that Ian had received the last rites, and so was very surprised and delighted – when Ian turned up at the House of Bishops' meeting in York a week later!*

May 2009:

> *These updates are getting progressive, like the mesothelioma! In a recent update we asked you to join us in prayer that we might "go with the flow" and accept God's timing and plans for us. That is easier said than done. The flow is now clearly downhill, and at a fairly rapid rate; the journey's end is probably in sight. So do pray that we may push the boundaries again, just a little, and that Ian will manage St Peter's Day which could be a celebration that will give wonderful closure to our time here in Peterborough and indeed to nearly 40 years of ministry.*

Food for the Journey

Usually it is no good starting on an energetic and demanding journey without having given due thought to food and meals, drinks and snacks. However, as we started on this particular journey we were not giving any conscious thought to it; God as guide and quartermaster intervened! Constantly along the way there were "God moments" when I was aware that he was speaking, or that we were being given some gift or resource to cheer us on our way. There were spiritual riches, services attended, liturgy heard afresh, bible-reading insights, Lambeth Conference moments, cell-group sharing, but also practical and mundane events and so many other ways in which God's presence seemed very real and relevant.

We should never underestimate the power of the "word" of God, and the various ways in which it comes to us. God finds so many means to "speak" to us in ways that each of us, as individuals, resonate with: it may be through daily bible reading; through the liturgy in church; through the things said or written by other people; through observing the world around us. It is through keeping all our senses open and alert to the presence of God in his world, and expecting to see, hear, feel, touch, and even taste, that God can speak and make us aware of eternal realities beyond ourselves. And we do not always have to be too serious about this, because in our experience it was sometimes the humorous and the bizarre that was able to lighten up our perspective on God's world and on what he was doing in our lives.

Verbal riches

I can be like a magpie collecting treasures and riches (albeit verbal ones), and finding that familiar words can bring new and personal insights, or comfort, or inspiration. Time and again I would find that the emailed Word for the Week from the LCF was speaking directly to me, and I was grateful to my legal colleagues who chose the verses and wrote the comments. They could not know how relevant or timely their comments on Bible passages might be, yet they had brought comfort as we waited for the results of tests and the initial diagnosis, and they helped me as I tried to absorb the uncertainties of the journey we were on.

Likewise I valued the use of scripture in the form of canticles in the morning worship that Ian and I shared in The Palace chapel, and I found the daily recitation of the verses at the end of the Benedictus gently encouraging: "In the tender compassion of our God, the dawn from on high shall break upon us, to shine on those who dwell in darkness and the shadow of death, and to guide our feet into the way of peace." [15]

Familiar words in the liturgy and collects had the power to become personally relevant. In the autumn of 2008, as the landscape was changing again, I was struck by the Collect for the Eighteenth Sunday after Trinity: "Almighty and everlasting God, increase in us your gift of faith, that, forsaking what lies behind, and reaching out to that which is before, we may run the way of your commandments and win the crown of everlasting glory."[16] At times the language of the 1662 Book of Common Prayer has unrivalled depths. A more contemporary prayer in our diocesan prayer cycle also managed to hit the right note: "May God bless us with peace to calm our hearts, strength to support our weakness, faith to drive away our despair, life to fill our loneliness, and hope to conquer doubt."[17] And doubt, lurking but unacknowledged, was always hovering.

The "Thought for the Day" slot on the BBC Radio 4 *Today* programme sometimes spoke clearly. I remember Chief Rabbi Lord Jonathan Sacks talking about the Jewish festival of Succoth, or Tabernacles, when, in re-enactment of the biblical festival, Jewish people would leave the security of their houses and move into a temporary shack in the garden. He saw this as a "festival of insecurity", and talked about the importance of the "nail of faith" which would attach the flimsy shack to something more solid to withstand the storms of life. Now that illustration resonated with me at a time when we found ourselves living with insecurity, with uncertainty, with the concept of "when" not "if", and with a journey where the landscape and the terrain might change dramatically round the next corner.

And almost randomly, indeed prophetically, as we seemed to be approaching the end of the journey, the regular prayer diary booklet arrived from CMS with, on the back of it, a prayer that was so relevant it could have been written just for us:

> I give you praise, God of my journey,
> for the taste of the little dyings which have
> strengthened me for this moment,
> I give you thanks, God of my journey,
> for those who have always stood near me and given
> me spiritual energy.
> I ask forgiveness, God of my journey,
> for ignoring your voice when you urged me to let go,
> for fighting off the dying that is essential for
> growing.
> I beg assistance, God of my journey,
> to believe beyond this point, to look at the painful
> parts of my life,
> and to grow through them.[18]

Floral riches

We are so often encouraged to "say it with flowers", and indeed the beauty and the fragrance of flowers is lovely. As the landscape of our world changed again in the autumn of 2008, we were surrounded by wonderful gifts from loving friends. There were freesias from our Parcevall cell mates, yellow roses from our suffragan bishop's wife, a tiny posy of late flowering purple and white sweet peas from the garden of a local friend, a display of beautiful roses from one of the women clergy, and a maroon and green arrangement from the ladies at a parish where I had spoken recently about the Lambeth Conference. All were very special and visual tokens of love and caring.

Gastronomic riches

Food for the journey came in literal form as well. Throughout this journey there were many memorable meals. They still embody for me memories of place, of people, of occasion, of points of departure, and of resting points on the journey. The tangible in terms of food and drink becomes symbolic of the significance of each occasion. Everyone has their own aide-memoire in life: for some it may be through music; for some through pictures or photos; for some the memories of landscape or of flowers and gardens; and sometimes perhaps people or words are the trigger. I have always enjoyed food ever since my father sent me on a cordon bleu cookery course before university, because deep down he wanted a useful domesticated daughter and not an academic "blue stocking"! And there is something very biblical about the significance of shared meals which feature so often in both Old and New Testaments, from the Israelites gathering their impromptu meals of quail and manna in the wilderness, to the bread and wine of the Last Supper on the night before Jesus died.

So I can retrace my steps on this journey as I think about the meals, and I can mark the significant moments, laugh or cry at the memories, create my own virtual scrapbook of menus. Entries would include:

- That day in Harley Street, as we tried to absorb the shock of the diagnosis, we had walked round to the Wallace Collection, a calming cultural oasis. We had sampled their new café in the inner courtyard, which, echoing the British Museum, has been covered over with a glass roof, and we had a simple lunch of quiche and salad with a glass of wine to fortify our nerves.

- A week later, before the first significant meeting with the oncologist to discuss the details of the prognosis and treatment options, we had the Italian lunching experience at Carluccio's opposite Barts Hospital, and randomly met an old school friend of Ian's who remained unaware of the significance of the occasion for us.

- The next two visits to the clinic found us exploring the new St Pancras Station concourse and lunching at Le Pain Quotidien with another splendid salad, and then discovering at the British Library their lovely upstairs café with its wonderful soups and outside terrace, and the joy of walking past the central "tower" with George III's library beautifully displayed. This unexpected disruption of our life was offering opportunities for new discoveries in London.

- Before the first chemo treatment we stayed nearby
  with the Bishop of London, but since he and
  his wife were out that evening we dined locally
  at an Italian restaurant, seated at a table in the
  window, with the most stunning view of St Paul's
  Cathedral, wonderfully flood-lit on a winter's
  night. The meal brought back memories of our
  Advent weekend in Rome, with polenta con
  funghi, superb seafood linguini, panna cotta, and
  of course limoncello as a "digestif".

- Another night-before-chemo visit to the Bishop
  of London found us dining in the City at another
  branch of Le Pain Quotidien located in Bread Street,
  which seemed wonderfully appropriate. These
  highlights were important to counterbalance the
  actual experience of chemo treatment as Ian spent
  up to six hours on the hospital ward having things
  dripped into him and knowing that he would feel
  really rough for the next few days.

- Ian found one of the worst aspects of chemo was the
  effect on his sense of taste, so for a while food had
  no allure, and fine wine was rather wasted on him,
  although that did, of course, make abstinence in Lent
  much easier! Likewise Ian found that the lunchtime
  sandwiches on offer in the hospital chemo ward did
  nothing to encourage the appetite.

- A panic painting and decorating session at Lanehead
  before moving furniture up there was enlivened

by help from a long-standing friend who, having a good wine cellar, had arrived with a claret which complemented one that we had received as a Christmas present. A post-painting, recuperative, dinner turned into a wine tasting as we compared a chateau's first and second growths (Leoville Poyferré and Moulin Riche for the wine buffs!). Somehow, such moments and details matter and add an extra dimension to life.

- Attending General Synod for the last time in February 2009 Ian wisely took plenty of time out from the sessions and fitted in a couple of attendances at the House of Lords. On those occasions tea and anchovy toast in the Lords' dining room seemed much more tempting than the more mundane alternative on offer in Synod's temporary tea room at Church House!

- Dinner at Deene Park, Northamptonshire, in late April 2009 was one of our most memorable civic dinners, with a salmon mousseline and a ragout of venison, and a wonderful rendering of the "Charge of the Light Brigade", since Deene was the seat of the Cardigan family. Despite coming straight from York and a meeting of the House of Bishops, Ian was on good form and enjoyed the tour of the house with its mementos of the Crimean War, as well as meeting civic leaders and friends.

- The impromptu visit from Sussex friends for Ian's birthday in April 2009 led to us sharing an Indian takeaway and remembering many similar occasions in Sussex when we had celebrated birthdays in this way.

- The night before Ian died the family had gathered in Peterborough to absorb the dramatic change in the medical reports, and to plan for quality time together in the remaining weeks that we hoped lay ahead. I can still visualise us as we sat round the table and dined together, with, of course, a good bottle of claret (Moulin Riche again!).

Spiritual riches

Throughout the eighteen months of Ian's illness the "God moments" were many and varied, and I found that the words of a familiar hymn, with both its realism about our reluctance and spiritual blindness and its expectation of God's intervention, became very relevant: "Oh, speak and make me listen, thou guardian of my soul".

O let me hear thee speaking
in accents clear and still,
above the storms of passion,
the murmurs of self-will;
O speak to reassure me,
to hasten or control;
O speak and make me listen,
thou guardian of my soul.

John Ernest Bode[19]

***

Grace before a meal:

Most loving Father,
on whose bountiful providence we do wholly depend;
Give us daily at thy pleasure whatsoever
the necessity of this life requireth;
but above all feed our souls with spiritual food,
with the bread of life from heaven:
through Jesus Christ our Lord.

After Erasmus[20]

Pushing Boundaries

I enjoyed the mission statement adopted by Liverpool Cathedral during Justin Welby's time there as dean, which included the statement that "the Cathedral is a safe place to take risks in the service of Jesus Christ". It embodies the idea that Christian life and ministry are not meant to be safe, but we are asked to take risks, to dream dreams, to have a sense of vision, and to push at the boundaries. During Ian's illness he was always pushing boundaries. He was never prepared to accept limitations on what he could do or achieve; life was for living, and Christian ministry was there to be exercised to the full. I was reminded of a friend of mine whose motto in life was: "You take the opportunities of a lifetime in the lifetime of the opportunity."

After the end of the first course of chemo, when the medics were optimistic about the possibly longer survival time of two to three years, we allowed our horizons to broaden. We began to take a step back from total immersion in episcopal life and welcomed the thought that retirement might eventually become a reality. Since both the GP and the oncologist felt that the boundaries might have extended we were encouraged to think ahead positively. But how far? To our ruby wedding anniversary in September 2009? To Ian's sixty-fifth birthday in April 2010? To a sabbatical or some extended time out? To retirement?

And for better or for worse, and as an act of faith, I felt willing and able to increase my commitment to the PCT and to agree to become Vice-Chair and also to take over the chairmanship of the new arm's length "provider services" organisation. This was the result of the Labour government's decision to separate out commissioning and providing in the NHS (thus reinventing the wheel and going back to the market economy introduced by the Conservatives in the 1990s!). In theory this was to be a transitional stage and Peterborough Community Services would become an independent organisation within a reasonable time span, so that my commitment would be of limited duration. In the event it would certainly push my boundaries over the ensuing eighteen months. This bit of my public profile would stretch me, and would at times create conflicts of interest when Board meetings clashed with Ian's treatment schedules. On at least one occasion after chairing a meeting all morning I had to jump on a train to London to collect Ian from the chemo ward at Barts Hospital and accompany him home.

In the normal round of episcopal life Ian found that there were some priorities that could not be cancelled. The first course of chemo lasted from Christmas until, appropriately and amusingly, April Fool's Day, and during that time there were two important meetings at the Church Commissioners that Ian was determined to attend so that he could contribute to an agenda item on which he felt strongly. The first meeting came six days after a chemo session when he was still a bit below par so I travelled to London with him as his "minder". But the second one came only two days after a chemo session when he should have been tucked up in bed in Peterborough, so instead we stayed on in London with a doctor friend who lived close to Church House and, with determination and steroids, he was able to make the short journey to the meeting.

Lanehead always seemed to give Ian new energy, focus, and motivation, and he would indulge in surprisingly strenuous DIY. The projects for the spring of 2008 were to redesign the kitchen and convert the garage into a library, and so, during our post-Christmas holiday, together we demolished half the kitchen fittings and cleared the accumulated rubbish from the garage, including about a ton and a half of stone roofing slates!

After Easter, with post-chemo energy and enthusiasm, Ian and the children would assemble and fit a completely new IKEA kitchen, and then at the Whitsun holiday, with friends from Peterborough, he would lay a new wooden floor in the newly converted library. Ian was "at home" in Weardale and he could indulge a private passion for DIY, happily pushing himself to surprising limits and then enjoying the fruits of his labours. Painting walls, demolishing a porch, re-laying part of a stone flag floor, building bookshelves – all these were just challenges to be met and enjoyed. Why not?!

There were times when juggling the diary became quite comic as Ian tried to fit in random and disparate appointments. One week towards the end of the first course of chemo remains in my memory. Ian's blood count was dropping again and so was his energy, and for once Barts did not have the capacity to deal with a blood transfusion together with his chemo on the Tuesday, so instead we had to fix something up impromptu with the local hospital for Friday. Then, in the same week, there was an important memorial service in Kettering on the Thursday for one of the county's "great and good" whom Ian had known and respected and so very much wanted to attend. Meanwhile, the Church Commissioners had arranged the official handover of the new offices by the builders for Friday afternoon. Somehow this balancing act worked – the bishop was present for the important occasions, and the necessary medical treatment slotted in. As we told the oncologist, it is amazing what prayer, determination, and medical science can do – in roughly that order.

However, some pressures on the diary did ease since, with convenient timing, Ian's various commitments as Chair of the Council for Christian Unity, as President of Council for St John's College Durham, and as Joint Chair of the Joint Implementation Commission of the Anglican Methodist Covenant all came to an end in the summer of 2008. God's timing was good.

The Lambeth Conference came at a time when Ian

was feeling re-energised after his first course of chemo, had coped with the busy early summer programme and was able to indulge in three weeks of relentless conference activity. He paced himself carefully through the weeks so that he could participate fully in the things that mattered most to him, and it was worth the effort.

Once Ian had announced his retirement in the autumn of 2008, a degree of panic set in as we realised quite how many boundaries we were going to have to push in the coming year. Quite apart from sorting a lifetime of accumulated clutter at The Palace, we would have to finish the transformation at Lanehead, and decide on necessary work to be done to the Durham house when the students moved out at the end of the academic year. And for good measure, in France we had embarked on having the *chai*, or wine store, at courtyard level converted to provide a third bedroom and the inevitable *atelier*, or workshop, for Ian (something which puzzled the French because they don't go in for *petit bricolage* at all!).

The second course of chemo was just another challenge to be managed. Christmas 2008, with the BBC televising both our Midnight Communion and the Family Service on Christmas Day in Peterborough Cathedral, was a time to make an effort and ensure that although it was only five days after a chemo session Ian was sufficiently medicated and well enough to preside at Midnight. Then at the end of January again shortly after chemo and with the necessary mixture of steroids, blood transfusion, and determination, Ian had enough energy to be in York Minster, robed and

Portrait of Ian by Ben Davies-Jenkins.

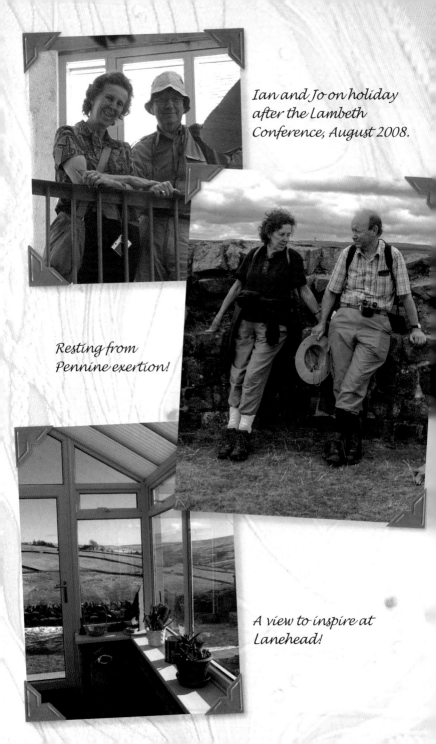

Ian and Jo on holiday after the Lambeth Conference, August 2008.

Resting from Pennine exertion!

A view to inspire at Lanehead!

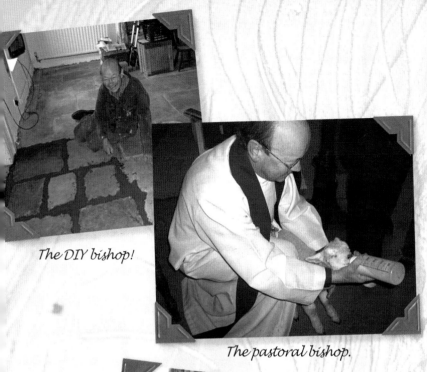

The DIY bishop!

The pastoral bishop.

Proud grandfather.

The "Cundy cope" in
Peterborough...

... and in Durham

The Palace at Peterborough.

The hall, ideal venue for a two piano "soirée".

The family at Christmas 2007.

Three generations.

The family at Paul and Sara's wedding in 2010.

Proud granny in Australia for the baptism.

The rural retreat at Lanehead.

Emerging from Christchurch Cathedral, NZ, after the earthquake on 22nd February 2011.

processing, for the consecration of the third successive Warden of Cranmer Hall to become a diocesan bishop. It was a very special and splendid occasion.

On a more private and cultural level, we visited the Byzantine exhibition at the Royal Academy and Ian found that a wheelchair was the perfect answer to the weariness of standing and walking round for long periods, but, of course, I was not allowed to push it! We even found time and energy, for a chilly, but good, long weekend in France, with some inevitable DIY with son Paul as our workmate and chief decorator.

Visiting Durham was always worth the effort, and in February 2009 St John's College celebrated its centenary. We were able to be present for the weekend, for the cathedral service, and then the splendid black-tie dinner followed by an amazing firework display on the riverbanks. Visiting London was more routine, though tiring, but Ian's last General Synod was also worth the effort and Archbishop Rowan's traditional farewell to retiring members of Synod was well researched, gently humorous, and very moving.

Pushing boundaries and living life to the full found its climax in the last week of Ian's life. We had come back from another wonderfully restorative weekend with our bishops' cell group at Parcevall Hall in Wharfedale, and then celebrated Ian's sixty-fourth birthday with a trip to London to an exhibition at Tate Britain, and an impromptu takeaway supper party with friends who called in while visiting family who lived locally.

The clinic appointment on Friday had been

disappointing, both because the computer technology was not working properly, and because, even so, the oncologist was clear from the written report on the CT scan that the cancer was progressing rapidly. But Ian still had life and energy and a vocation. So, on Saturday he confirmed twenty-seven students at Oakham School, mingled with parents and children afterwards, and stayed on for lunch at the headmaster's house.

On Sunday we hosted a private renewal of marriage vows for friends in the chapel at The Palace and welcomed them and their friends for a tea reception afterwards. On Monday we planned our "final fling" party at The Palace for our farewell in July. On Tuesday, after the GP had called and explained the sobering reality of the new prognosis and limited time span, we lifted our spirits by going to Cambridge for a service in Great St Mary's as part of the university's 800th centenary celebrations, and it was good to connect with familiar faces in familiar surroundings as we focused on the rich heritage of the teaching of theology over those centuries.

On Wednesday Ian went over to Northampton to receive the vows of one of his clergy, who was also a former student at Cranmer Hall, who was becoming a solitary religious. He did, however, cancel his attendance at the meeting of rural deans and lay chairs and instead came home for dinner with the family who had all gathered in Peterborough that day. And on Thursday morning we met with folk in the diocesan office to plan a farewell service and tea party for the retired clergy and widow(er)s in July.

It had been an extraordinarily full and varied week, with its highs and lows, its public and private moments. So we packed up and left by car for Somerset anticipating a relaxed and private weekend with family and friends, celebrating the ruby wedding anniversary of two of our oldest friends at Great Wood Camp in the Quantocks where they were married and where Ian used to go as a boy on summer camps. How many more boundaries can you push? How can life be more abundant and more fulfilling? And... how can God manage the unexpected yet again?

Pathways? Boundaries? Trust Ian to find a shortcut!

In Matthew 14:28–32 Peter "pushes the boundaries" and steps out in faith…

> *[Peter said:] "Lord, if it is you, bid me come to you on the water." [Jesus said:] "Come". So Peter got out of the boat and walked on the water and came to Jesus; but when he saw the wind, he was afraid, and beginning to sink he cried out, "Lord, save me." Jesus immediately reached out his hand and caught him, saying to him, "O man of little faith, why did you doubt?" And when they got into the boat, the wind ceased.*

* * *

Make the omnipotence of God the measure of your expectation.

Adapted from James W. Alexander, 1852, quoted on a prayer plaque owned by Ian's cousin, Mary Cundy

Part Two

*A second "determining moment". It is 6 p.m. on
7 May 2009. I am sitting in the car in Marlborough
High Street, one hand still on the steering wheel,
the other holding Ian's hand, but I know that he has
just died. He has suddenly and simply slipped away.
I feel numb. I ring my GP practice in Peterborough
and a patient but firm voice keeps saying, "Jo, call an
ambulance." Obvious, really, but I am too shocked and
panicked to think the obvious.*

Grieving in Public

There were many scenarios that I had imagined but this wasn't one of them! Ian had not relished the prospect of a slow and painful downhill path, and in typical style he had found a shortcut to reach journey's end. The boat had been gently pulled to shore, and "all the trumpets [had] sounded for him on the other side".[21] But I was alone in Marlborough with an ambulance crew intent on doing the full resuscitation procedures before finally admitting defeat and taking us to Swindon Hospital. It was evening, it was dark, and on arrival at hospital the place felt so cold and clinical, but the chaplain was on hand and doing a good job at coping with a bereaved and shocked bishop's wife, even getting hold of the local suffragan bishop to come and see me.

Back in Peterborough the news was gradually spreading because I had been able to contact the wife of our own suffragan bishop by phone. And our GP, who over the years had become a good friend to our family as well as a trusted medical adviser, had gone to The Palace and broken the news to Paul and Liz, and then phoned Robert who had returned to Leeds that afternoon. The practical problem of getting me back to Peterborough was also solved by our GP who arranged to drive to Swindon to collect me, bringing with him Liz, and also his brother-in-law who, as an ex-police driver, would be able to drive Ian's car back from Marlborough. Paul was left to hold the fort at The Palace, to make other urgent phone calls, and to make beds for Robert, Susan, and baby Thor. It was after midnight when I arrived home. There were no words, just tears and hugs.

Already the tom-toms were beating! The news would spread fast and publicly. That night it even spread across the Atlantic to the West Indies where Archbishop Rowan was attending a meeting of the Anglican Consultative Council, and by 9 o'clock the next morning a beautiful handwritten letter from him had arrived by fax. It was the first of many, but remains for me the most special and moving. Then that day, with the speed of modern communications, emails were sent around the diocese and relevant parts of the Church of England, and a press release was drafted and sent out. By lunchtime the media were covering the story on local radio and television, and the local press were preparing their coverage.

For the diocese this was an immense shock, this sudden death being something for which they were wholly unprepared. The senior staff were also stunned, and as they each came and visited we could share our bemused grief, and cry on each other's shoulders. In a curious way there was a sense in which the support was mutual. Inevitably, and wonderfully, we received a veritable deluge of cards and letters, the postman struggling with bundles of 100 or more each day. They came from friends, from parishioners, from colleagues in the church, in Parliament, in the NHS, in the law, in ecumenical, academic and university circles, from civic bodies, and also from people with whom we had not been in contact for years, if not decades. The fragrance of flowers filled the house, and simple gifts of home-made cakes, etc. arrived. It was both humbling and affirming, and we were indeed almost "overwhelmed by the family of fellowship who mourned Ian's passing", as one friend wrote.

The public and private sides of our lives merged as obituaries appearing in the press paid tribute to the many and varied aspects of this man who had been my husband, my beloved "holy polymath"! One of the best and most concise appreciations appeared later in the *College Record* for St John's College, Durham:

> Ian Cundy will be remembered by his friends and family for many things – his delight in fine wine, vintage cars, old clocks, and DIY; his hospitality; his passion for ecumenism; his peaceful and gentle presence; his warm and welcoming smile; his constancy. Yet his greatness lay in his calling to be a servant – of St John's College, of the Church of England, and of the wider people of God. And all this flowed out of his utter conviction that God loved him, and would not let him go.[22]

A report from the Coroner's Officer on the initial result of the post-mortem was helpful in revealing that the cancer had spread to the abdominal cavity and that Ian had died when one of the tumours had haemorrhaged. It was good to know, in some measure, why it had been so quick and simple, and that there was nothing that could have been done to stop it. It helped to bring one element of closure.

Three days after Ian died, I felt brave enough, supported by the children and close friends, to join the cathedral congregation for the Sunday Eucharist. It felt important to be there and to share my grief and shock with theirs, to pray together, to cry together, to join in the familiar words of the liturgy, to reach out to God's presence, to seek peace and hope.

However, although Ian had always confidently told me that I would cope when I was on my own, I was aware now that I was in a dream world. I am by nature an achiever, a perfectionist, trained to cope, but suddenly I had been pushed beyond my personal limits – physical, emotional, and spiritual. Early in our marriage Ian had stretched my hitherto meagre hiking abilities by taking us up Scafell Pike in the Lake District, saying that he wanted to know what happened when I was pushed beyond my limits! Well, now in a very different context I was finding that out again! In the rather erudite psychological language of Myers–Briggs it seemed that I was living in my "Jungian shadow", that I was not just "out of my comfort zone", but that my normal ways of functioning and reacting were suspended, and I was "another person" trying to cope with this sense of unreality.

Fortunately, the children had stepped into this void and

taken over the running of the domestic side of Palace life, doing the shopping and organising meals, and ensuring that we had quality time together on our own. And in the midst of all this it was the mundane crises of life that kept our feet on the ground – the fridge was dying, Liz's garden was a disaster of weeds, our private email domain was down because Ian hadn't renewed the subscription for it, and we didn't know the password for his House of Lords' laptop.

Decisions! We had learned to live with the fact that Ian could not have a private illness, and we knew that now the same would apply to his funeral and that it would be a very public farewell. So we found ourselves having to cope with all the many details and arrangements that had to be decided. The timing was fixed to coincide with the end of a residential meeting of the House of Bishops which was happening close by in Leicestershire, so that there was opportunity for attendance by both the archbishops, and as many bishops as could clear their diaries. Ian had already written the whole of his funeral service in detail, so it was only necessary for the choir to learn the music he had chosen and for decisions to be made about participants.

But, of course, much more needed to be done. We had to send out details of the funeral arrangements to friends and family, and circulate details more widely; we had to sort out seating, decide on appropriate refreshments, and on flowers, and even think about mundane things like parking. In all of this Ian's office staff were wonderfully practical and efficient, doing most of the work, liaising inevitably with the press and media, and being very good at gently organising me.

And the children had also taken over the role of "mother's minder", so that I was always accompanied by one of them to meetings to ensure that in the complexity of it all we did actually have agreement about the decisions made.

Most importantly, we needed as a family to protect our own privacy and space, while welcoming the many others from so many areas of our life who wanted to come and share in this farewell service. We needed to be able to grieve in private and it required careful planning. So we decided that while the funeral service was a public occasion, the burial in the cathedral precincts would be private, and that afterwards there would be a reception at The Palace for a limited number of invited friends and family, while the rest of the congregation were entertained in the cathedral. Also private would be the reception of the coffin into the cathedral on the night before the funeral with a small and intimate gathering of family and close friends, together with some members of the cathedral congregation. The liturgy was simple and the music sung by the small chamber choir with which Liz normally sang, one anthem being a Celtic prayer in a lovely setting written for Ian by Christopher Gower, the former Master of the Music:

> May the road rise to meet you,
> May the wind be always at your back,
> May the sun shine warm upon your face,
> May the rains fall softly upon your fields,
> And until we meet again
> May God hold you in the hollow of his hand.[23]

It was a time for quiet prayer and tears, for hugs and silent support, to be unhurried in our very personal farewells. And the next morning, before the afternoon funeral, there was opportunity for people to return to the peace of the cathedral chancel, with the coffin lying there draped with Ian's cope, surrounded by four tall, lit candles, and beneath it a floral arrangement in the shape of an Ichthyan fish, the early Christian symbol and a reminder of the choir where Ian and I had met in our university days. I went and knelt in the choir stalls, knowing that Ian was at peace, at home in his cathedral, and that we were together.

The funeral itself was indeed public, and splendid, and moving, and in a wonderful sense, triumphant. It was Ian's last act of priestly ministry and an affirmation of his Christian faith as expressed in his own introduction to the service:

> I invite you in this service to contemplate the mystery of God, in the light of which I have sought to live my life and understand its meaning. That mystery is proclaimed in the natural world around us, for which I have a deep and lasting affection, in the record of God's dealings with his people and uniquely in the coming of Jesus, the Christ, in whose service I have tried to be faithful from the days when I learnt the meaning of faith from my parents to the privilege and responsibility of priestly and episcopal ministry. Accepting that pattern of disciplined living has brought me much joy, plenty of hard work, and

a rich variety of friends – not least my wife, my
family and my colleagues… Life's journey takes
us from the known past and present into the
unknown future, strengthened by those visions
of God and his presence which come to us in a
variety of ways through our own experience as
well as the rich insights of others. My prayer is
that perhaps in a small way this service may prove
one of those moments of encounter which sustain
and encourage us and makes every Eucharist a
transforming experience as the ordinary becomes
the extra-ordinary and the stuff of life becomes the
vehicle of the divine presence among us.

There were memorable moments. A heart-stopping moment
as we, the family, arrived at the west door, preceded by a
verger, and the entire congregation of 1,300 people rose to
their feet, and Robert held my hand tightly as we led the
family procession down the aisle. A moment of liturgical
splendour as the clergy processed in including both
archbishops and about forty bishops in their red chimeres.
Informal moments as one of the bishops gently touched my
arm as he passed by, and as Archbishop Sentamu laid his
hand on the coffin in his own personal tribute of farewell.
Musical moments including the haunting "Funeral Ikos" by
John Tavener as the coffin was finally taken out. Historic
moments since Ian was the first diocesan bishop to die in
office for over twenty-five years, and also this was the first
time since the year 970 that both archbishops had been in

Peterborough Cathedral together.[24]

And the media were there. This was a big public event and there was coverage on local radio and television and in the local papers. There were benefits from this in that it allowed people across the diocese to feel some sense of involvement in this "rite of passage" even if they had not been able to attend.

And afterwards. The outpouring of love and support and sympathy had been a wonderful cushion on which to rest, and the funeral service had been a focal point in the finality of "journey's end". But reality needed to be faced. There are not many situations that put such stress on a bereaved spouse and family as the death of a clergy person in office. The tied accommodation syndrome meant that, at a stroke, I was losing not only my husband, but my home, my church, my friends, my NHS role. In these situations time is of the essence, and the requirement to pack up and go comes with a fairly limited timeframe. The only bonus for me was that we had already thought about it and planned towards imminent retirement, so much of the decision-making was done, though the time scales might need to be adjusted.

And the normal world was demonstrating its habit of reasserting it demands. Within days of the funeral my NHS commitments were impinging themselves. We had the green light to go ahead with new appointments to the PCS Board, which would eventually relieve me of responsibility, but in other leadership areas there was the potential for lively conflict and challenge and I could see my role as Vice-Chair of the PCT becoming more demanding than I either wanted or needed. Then on the family front, Liz had gone ahead with planned minor surgery on the weekend after the funeral, and then for good measure had some tricky dental treatment a week later, and she was likely to be off work for two or three weeks and needing TLC. However, there was a bonus aspect in that during her convalescence Liz had time to begin to sort out and list all the hundreds of cards and letters that I had received.

The momentum of life at The Palace continued. In one sense this helped because there were routine things to be done and to be organised. In another sense it hindered because I could postpone the really difficult decisions and actions that needed to be addressed. In June the senior staff held their regular meeting at The Palace for the last time, and at lunchtime I was able to give to each of them the wonderful pottery gifts that Ian and I had chosen together in Alston at Easter. St Peter's Day would come at the end of June. It was an occasion I had always loved: the cathedral's patronal festival and a big diocesan celebration, with its garden party and festival evensong – an occasion for hats and cream teas, sunshine, and roses. Ian and I had intended that it would mark our retirement, but now it had become the occasion for my solo farewell to the diocese, and the service had become a thanksgiving for Ian's life and ministry, in the very appropriate context of celebrating the life and ministry of St Peter. It was another big public occasion.

In another of those compromises between the private and the public, we had a bring-and-share picnic lunch in the garden for the many friends and family coming from afar before the formal public proceedings started on St Peter's Day. The sun shone and the atmosphere throughout the day was of thanksgiving and celebration. It was a time of gifts – the gift of several very personal tributes to Ian delivered during the service, and then the parting gifts to me from the diocese, including a book which had been compiled with contributions from each of the parishes encapsulating in wonderful variety a record of life and faith across the diocese. It was a time for me to express my thanks to the diocese for all that Ian and I had been able to share with them over thirteen years, and to thank them for their love, support, and prayers during our pilgrimage through Ian's illness. It was a time to look back and a time to look forward; a time to thank God for his goodness. *Mungu yu mwema* – God is good, all the time!

However, my life would not be same without the unexpected and the bizarre. On the evening before St Peter's Day it was Paul who was suffering acute abdominal pains and needed an urgent trip to the NHS Walk-in Centre, receiving the same stop-gap advice of painkillers and referral to the GP as Liz had previously received on Boxing Day.

But St Peter's Day was not quite my last public occasion in the diocese. In July there was still the evensong and tea party for the retired clergy and widow(er)s which Ian and I had been planning on the morning of the day he died, and now I attended it alone and bade them farewell as a clergy widow myself. The role of "bishop's wife" was past, and now, at last, I could no longer postpone turning my mind to the more private, and increasingly urgent, matter of moving!

113

Into the darkness and warmth of the earth
we lay you down.
Into the sadness and smiles of our memories
we lay you down.
Into the cycle of living and dying and rising again
we lay you down.

Into the freedom of wind and sunshine
we let you go.
Into the dance of the stars and the planets
we let you go.
Into the wind's breath and the hands of the star maker
we let you go.

Ruth Burgess[25]

Alone with God

How do you express the sense of loss that comes with any bereavement? It is unique, individual, relative to its own context, something which each person experiences alone in their own way. Perhaps it is summed up in those heart-breaking words of Greek myth as Orpheus mourns Eurydice: "What is life to me without you? What is left if you are dead?"[26]

For me that first, almost sleepless, night was a new journey into unknown territory. I was alone – alone in our shared bed; alone when I woke; alone as I began a new day; alone when the day ended and Ian was not there as I dropped into bed again – and a hot water bottle is a poor substitute! I felt bereft, like a bird without a wing, and yet alive in the "here and now", conscious that I still had the continued gift of life. Nothing had prepared me, nothing had told me that there would be such a void, such emptiness, such numbness. Over the ensuing days tears would flow only rarely, usually in the early mornings when I woke alone, or as I read through some of each day's mountain of cards

.rt was the honest facing of reality.
,sorb and rely on Ian's philosophy
ance and peace, his acceptance and
ɔ grieve and yet to hope, to find a way
sing to God what I was feeling.

between Ian's death and his funeral
became a   ecial time. All three of our children had
been able to arrange for time off work, and we were able to
spend quality time together absorbing the reality of what
had happened, learning to adjust to life without Ian, to the
change in family dynamic, and coping individually and
corporately with our grief. I needed that space and time
to begin to unravel the complexity of my own responses –
physical, emotional, and spiritual. At times I could be on
"auto-pilot", and at other times wholly "adrift".

The funeral sermon by our suffragan bishop was simply
and beautifully constructed around the words which Ian
and I had prayed together each morning in the chapel at
The Palace: "The night has passed, the day lies open before
us, let us pray with one heart and mind."[27] And he was
right, because one journey had ended, the "night" of Ian's
illness had passed, and another journey, another day, was
opening up ahead. They were words for me to hang on to,
to continue to pray daily.

The funeral was Ian's final and wonderful gift to us
all. It was a service to remember and treasure, and he had
spoken through it so clearly and positively. But picking
up the threads of life after it was easier said than done. I
found myself physically, mentally, and emotionally tired;

spiritually drained. Motivation was a problem and I realised that I would need a "phased" return to whatever might count for "normality".

I began to realise that perhaps the key was the concept of acceptance which Ian and I had come to experience over the last eighteen months. We had accepted the reality, the losses, the loneliness, and the pain; we had each come to terms with them and learned to accommodate them. It had been a matter of learning to "go with the flow", even if we didn't understand, and even if it stretched faith to the limits.

As I struggled with this, one of Ian's fellow bishops sent me a lovely letter with a complicated but profound quotation from theologian Dietrich Bonhoeffer:

> [In] the absence of someone whom we love... the need is to simply hold out and see it through... it is nonsense to say that God fills the gap; God does not fill it, but on the contrary God keeps it empty and so helps us keep alive our former communion with each other, even at the cost of pain... the dearer and richer the memories, the more difficult our separation. But gratitude changes the pangs of memory into tranquil joy. The beauties of the past are borne, not as a thorn in the flesh, but as a precious gift in themselves.[28]

In the void that I was experiencing, I had to believe that time, and God, would truly change the pain and the pangs of memory into tranquil joy.

And into the void came the curious and unexpected

experience of a friend within the diocese. This wonderfully down-to-earth deaconess, not normally given to visions, shared with her vicar and then more widely that she had dreamt about Ian on the night that he died. She had seen him, together with me, sitting in a group of people and then receding in a blaze of light, and she had woken wondering why on earth she should dream about her bishop! To me it is still one of those amazing, random, prophetic, moments of revelation by God that bring a sense both of comfort and of mystery.

At times I felt overwhelmed by the job in hand and all the decisions that needed to be taken, the work that needed to be done both in clearing The Palace, and in making the houses in Durham and Weardale properly habitable. I felt alone, rather stressed, and vulnerable. And yet I was also aware of other people around me who needed my care and support. Robert and Susan were still adjusting to the demands of parenthood; Paul was facing the challenge of moving to Australia; a friend was moving into sheltered accommodation and I was acting as her attorney in the complicated sale of her house which was becoming a long-running saga; other friends needed a listening ear as they coped with caring for an elderly parent. Sara had arrived from Australia for a two-week holiday (and yes, I did recognise her!), and she and Paul needed my time and attention as they looked forward to and planned for their future. The network of relationships and need did not go away.

Where was the time to grieve? That the bereaved need time to grieve may sound obvious, but it is not always easy, and different people react in different ways. For some they may be in a state of shock where reality refuses to sink in, while for others, like me, there is just a daily necessity to keep going and to put on a brave face for the sake of the family, the diocese, one's colleagues. Life for me had continued to have pace and momentum. Both Paul and Liz were based now in Peterborough, frequent visitors at The Palace, and frequently hopeful of being fed and watered.

By this time I had had almost three months of constant activity and very little time to stop and reflect. Life had gone on but I was struggling to find personal focus. I needed a break; I needed time to get away from The Palace and its daily routine, and there was a God-given opportunity to join Liz who had decided to go with a pilgrimage group from Durham to spend a week at the Community of Taizé in France. I hoped this would be an opportunity to find time to stop and reflect, to pray, and actually to listen to God.

And Taizé was a watershed for me. I was alone with God, without distractions, in a wholly new environment that was focused entirely on seeking to explore faith and personal encounter with God and to open that up at every level – personal, social, intellectual, musical, spiritual. The context was a large communal site that "buzzed" with about 4,500 young people and about 500 "geriatrics" over the age of thirty-five years, and with a multitude of languages. The daily routine was organised round prayers in the church three times a day, and bible studies and discussion groups which were organised in age groups. Liz camped with her group and was my emergency lifeline, while I was accommodated in the guest house and cosseted by the Community.

Bible studies for the "geriatrics" in the mornings were led by one of the Brothers who had a wonderfully fresh exploration of the Gospel of Mark. For the rest of the day worship and meals provided the framework, and I rapidly realised that there was a limit to the number of new people that I could cope with meeting and talking to because I was feeling too fragile and vulnerable for such encounters. So I opted out of the discussion groups and enjoyed the luxury of having time for quiet and silent reflection, exploring the site and sitting in a field, or by the lake, or in the orchard. Alone I could lie on the sun-lit grass and water it with my tears. I also opted out of the social pressure created by communal meals and ate with the smaller group at the guest house. Above all I relished the silence that was built into all the worship, the gentle meditative nature of the chants, and the unity of this vast community of (mostly) young people exploring the gospel of Christ.

In fact the bible studies struck deep and painful depths, and I realised that I had to go through a process that had been on hold for three months. I needed to grieve, to cry, to accept, to explore, to enter new and unknown territory. Words from Isaiah spoke to me: "I am the Lord, I have called you in righteousness. I have taken you by the hand and kept you" (Isaiah 42:6). And I found myself praying, "God, open me up to face the past, the present, and the future – but please don't let go of me!" The process felt so risky, and I was trusting God to be faithful and to keep me.

So in various ways the Gospel of Mark was the catalyst that helped me to work through the process. In the same way that the person, identity, and ministry of Jesus are only gradually revealed in this particular gospel, and the disciples' understanding of this is equally gradual and slow, so I was learning that some things cannot be hurried and that grief was one of them. And particular passages acquired a new significance.

As we looked at the parable of the sower, and other parables about seed and harvest, I found myself thinking that Ian had been "ripe for harvest"; that he had been a remarkable person and that the last two years had been a remarkable time. There was a sense in which I did not want to lose sight of what he had lived and taught and shared, and I felt myself to be almost a trustee of his legacy, like the farmer who tends the sown field.

The feeding of the 5,000 had particular significance in the context of Taizé where one feels that this miracle is still taking place three times a day. But it was not the generosity and abundance of what Jesus provided that struck me so forcefully, but rather Brother Rob's exploration of the aftermath of the miracle in 6:43: "and they took up twelve baskets full of broken pieces".

Why are the scraps, the leftovers, collected? Why are they not thrown to the birds? What is their significance? Indeed these small insignificant scraps appear three times in this gospel: here in chapter 6; again in 8:8; after the feeding of the 4,000 ("they took up the broken pieces left over, seven baskets full"); and in chapter 7:27–28 when Jesus is talking to the Syrophoenician woman and says, "it is not right to take the children's bread and throw it to the dogs". She replies, "Yes, Lord; yet even the dogs under the table eat the children's crumbs."

The scraps are important, they are precious, and you cannot control the scraps, the crumbs; they escape and fall to places you do not notice or expect. And suddenly I found myself contemplating the reality and theology of the scrap, the leftover. Bereft as I felt, I began to ask myself whether I was in fact precious as the scrap left from the rich years of marriage, as the leftover of an abundant shared life of ministry? Was this the paradox of the gospel, of faith, that what is insignificant and left over is precious to God?

As we read of the healing of blind Bartimaeus we explored aspects of prayer: the need to open up to God's gift of mercy; to come with open hands; to explore what it is that God wants to give us, and to ask what God wants of us. These were challenging questions for me. They required real honesty as I found myself challenged to pray for discernment about my future. What did I want? What did God want?

Friday at Taizé is the day of the Cross, and as our bible study looked at the Passion of Jesus and considered the different people and groups who entered into a relationship with Jesus, it was Simon of Cyrene whose story struck me, the man for whom the cross became a burden that he had not chosen, but something that he carried on the road with Jesus beside him. On this Friday Archbishop Rowan was visiting Taizé and had been invited to celebrate an Anglican

Eucharist at the midday prayers. Archbishop Sentamu was also present, having joined the Durham and York group with whom Liz and I had come.

And suddenly… the memories came flooding back; my mind went back to Peterborough Cathedral, to Ian's funeral service, to having both archbishops present and Rowan presiding at the Eucharist. Emotion and grief poured out and I shed all the tears that I did not shed at the funeral. The floodgates opened and I sobbed uncontrollably through the whole service. Somehow Taizé feels a safe place in which to fall apart, and an unknown neighbour gently touched my shoulder and promised to pray for me. Afterwards Liz and a couple of her friends appeared and gently put me back together again.

I had at last faced the depths of my grief, that deep anguish of the broken-hearted. I had let go. And even now God had a gentle sense of humour – the cleaning team moved into the church with the hoover and the peace and quiet were abruptly shattered and I was brought down to earth. I felt exhausted, but I had a wonderful sense of release. God had not let go of me; he had been faithful, and he had kept me.

And now I had to leave Taizé, and I had to go back. Our final bible study focused on the resurrection story with the women going to the tomb and finding the young man sitting there who tells them, "go, tell his disciples and Peter that he [Jesus] is going before you to Galilee; there you will see him, as he told you" (Mark 16:7). Galilee was the place where everything had started for the disciples, and they were being invited to go back there to find Jesus again. So for us, as we prepared to leave Taizé, we were being called to return to our "Galilee" – to the places we had come from; to the place of our daily lives; and like the disciples we would go to find Jesus in our ordinary lives. So I had to step out in faith, to return to my Galilee, to trust that Jesus was ahead of me and fulfilling his promises to me.

Sunday at Taizé is "changeover" day, and this was the second Sunday on which I was invited to join other guests for lunch with the brothers. Meals had been an interesting feature of the week, the general fare for the young (and the not-so-young) pilgrims being extremely basic and simple, consisting generally of anything that could be eaten with a spoon from a bowl, and very reliant on pasta, rice, lentils, and other basic carbohydrates, with hidden nuggets of vegetable and meat! The brothers live equally simply, but this Sunday was a feast day to celebrate the life vows of a new brother from Senegal. So there were over 100 of us outside on the terrace at a long table decorated with African fabrics, and enjoying salad and grilled fish, wine, fruit and ice cream, and wonderful hot-roasted groundnuts which the new brother's family had brought with them from Senegal.

Taizé had been a watershed experience for me, and provided lots of everything – people, prayer, peace, space, silence, relaxation, sunshine, rain, and tears. It was my springboard for moving on, and I left it on a high.

Memories of Taizé

"See I am near" says the Lord,
"See I make all things new."

Taizé chant[29]

"I am the Lord, your Holy One,
the Creator of Israel, your King."
Thus says the Lord, who makes a way in the sea,
a path in the mighty waters...
"Remember not the former things,
nor consider the things of old.
Behold, I am doing a new thing;
now it springs forth, do you not perceive it?
I will make a way in the wilderness and rivers in the
desert...
to give drink to my chosen people,
the people whom I formed for myself,
that they might declare my praise.

Isaiah 43:15–21

Jésus le Christ, lumière intérieure
ne laisse pas mes ténèbres me parler.
Jésus le Christ, lumière intérieure,
Donne-moi d'accueillir ton amour.

Lord Jesus Christ, your light shines within us
let not my fears nor my doubts speak to me.
Lord Jesus Christ, your light shines within us,
let my heart always welcome your love.

Taizé chant[30]

Moving On

It was August and on the doorstep of The Palace were two friends laden with black bags and boxes whose mission was to focus and direct my hitherto butterfly nature, to banish procrastination, and to make me start the real and urgent challenge of packing. They were ruthless but loving, and ensured that by the end of that day I had started the necessary process of sorting and radical downsizing. They also made me realise that in order to maintain any sort of momentum I would need to have the company of a "dragon", or "slave-driver", or "gofer" on hand to help and encourage me. I also needed to set a line in the sand and have a timetable and so I booked removers for the beginning of September, come hell or high water!

Living in a "tied Palace" meant that, like other bereaved clergy spouses in tied accommodation, I needed to move out within a limited time span. This is part of the sacrifice and cost that comes with a life in ministry. But it is hard, and goes against the received wisdom that the bereaved need to have time to adjust before they make any major changes in their lives. I did not have the comfort of being able to cocoon myself in familiar surroundings and familiar routines any longer, and I envied those who could nurse their grief without the added trauma of moving. Nothing in my life was remaining stable and unchanged. I had the advantage that we had already thought about and planned towards retirement, so much of the decision-making was done, but the timescales needed to be adjusted, and the practicalities had to be faced.

Moving is always a hassle, and moving on one's own, as I was to find, is an impossible hassle. I had no idea it would be so awful. So many decisions needed to be made: what to keep; what to sell; what to recycle; what to throw away, etc. I needed so many boxes, so many bags, so many lists, and, of course, a large skip. And it would not be a tidy clean break on removal day because I knew that there would be unfinished business which I would need to come back and deal with. On a practical level there would need to be a final clearing up and sorting out of things still awaiting a destination, and fortunately Paul and Liz would still be on hand in Peterborough to help me cope with that. At a more professional level, I would attend my last NHS meetings at the end of September, going to the AGM for the PCT, and then handing over of chairmanship of PCS to a newly appointed Chair. I would be completing ten years of non-executive involvement.

All farewells are important – they are thresholds opening up the unknown future, and they need to be marked in some way. My final departure from Peterborough was no exception, marking as it did the closure of a complete chapter of my life lived in the context of marriage and ministry, and the beginning of a more solo way of life. So on my final weekend we decided to have a party at The Palace with fireworks – "Jo goes out with a bang!" – and friends and neighbours gathered. It was quite appropriate really as I thought back to the Guy Fawkes weekend in 2007 when we were preparing for the public announcement of Ian's illness. Then, after the Sunday Eucharist in the cathedral, there was cake and coffee and a few parting words.

So after two days of packing up and one day of unloading I arrived in Durham, with too much furniture and too many boxes and patient, but incredulous, removal men: "You mean you haven't got a garage?!" Friends down the road offered me a bed for a few days while I tackled the enormous task of unpacking and finding space to stand, sit, or sleep.

In the next week life was to prove eventful, again. My new car was broken into in the private car park underneath my friends' house, my new IKEA larder cupboard fell off the wall fully laden, and I succumbed to a very nasty gastric bug. I thought of a wry quotation that I had come across some years earlier and in moments of crisis had pinned to the noticeboard in my study at Peterborough: "Out of the gloom a voice said unto me, 'Smile and be happy, things might be worse' – so I smiled and was happy, and behold, things did get worse!" Many a true word spoken in jest.

But nothing had quite prepared me for the reality of moving and arriving in a new place. Beneath the constant wave of necessary activity there lurked a deep sense of disorientation, lack of motivation, and lack of any framework for life. I realised that my life was in a state of total dislocation and total disruption. The emptiness and the void were accentuated and no amount of pretty or practical details made up for that. Shortly after the move someone asked me, "Do you have your head above water?", and I replied, "Not really, but I am not drowning, and I have a lifeboat down the road with friends." Actually, I felt even more totally adrift and "at sea" than I had in the week after Ian had died.

Getting sorted was just such a major exercise and I found myself stuck in a quagmire of practicalities, not to mention paperwork, fearful that I would muddle on forever in a sea of packing boxes. Lurking below the surface was a loss of motivation – did it matter? Why bother? I was tired of coping and tired of not coping. Decision-making needs to be a shared experience not least so that taking either the credit or the blame can also be shared. I am a relational person, but I had no person to relate to, deeply, intimately, unreservedly; no person with whom to share the journey as a trusted, constant, daily travelling companion; no alter ego. In this situation one finds that friends and family tend to have their own commitments and cannot fill this role. I was hitting the mystery of life, of identity, of individuality, of personal worth, of purpose, and these eventually come down to issues of faith – not the motions of religion, but the reality of beliefs. I was caught between those God-moments of encounter with the divine, and a numb void without emotion or meaning.

Small things mattered. As I sorted the unpacking I had the diversion and the joy of unearthing forgotten treasures, be they books, papers, jotted notes, or quotations. In a drawer of Ian's desk I found a tiny old and faded newspaper cutting, sufficiently precious for him to have copied it out onto a piece of card. It was a quotation from Matthew Arnold and felt like a window into Ian's inner thoughts, feelings, and beliefs. It summed up so much of his philosophy of life:

> Is it so small a thing,
> to have enjoy'd the sun,
> to have lived light in the spring,
> to have loved, to have thought, to have done… ?[31]

I wanted to respond, "Is it so small a thing to have done all this, together?", and I felt less alone.

But in this "curate's egg" phase of my life, not all of it was bad and some parts of it were really quite good. Paul and Liz had joined me for the weekend of our ruby wedding anniversary, and although I was struggling with my gastric bug it was good to mark that milestone together. Then a significant highlight was a memorial service for Ian in Durham Cathedral at Michaelmas, which also marked the fortieth anniversary of his ordination as a deacon. And in this "ruby" year we celebrated after the service with a "ruby" cake made and iced by Ian's former secretary. Durham also had a lot to offer in terms of occupational therapy with lectures, dinners, church services, and other events. I was surrounded by friends old and new, and was cared for, loved, and looked after. As one friend wisely advised me, "Jo, you have status and sympathy – make the most of it!" That indeed was a great privilege and a great blessing, and a curious legacy of the public side of our life.

So we moved on through the autumn into the season of All Saints or "Toussaints" in France, where their shops are awash with colourful potted chrysanthemums to be taken to the graves of the faithful departed, and Liz and I brought our own tribute back after a half-term break in the Touraine, placing splendid purple flowers on Ian's grave. I was struck by words from the canticle for morning prayer in this season of the year: "Remember not the former things, nor consider the things of old. Behold, I am doing a new thing; now it springs forth, do you not perceive it?" (Isaiah 43:18–19). I realised that I had in fact detached myself from Peterborough and had no desire to go back there, to The Precincts, to The Palace, or to the Cathedral. Maybe because that part of my life – "the things of old" – was really finished and past; maybe because there was a reaction to the immense effort involved in packing up and clearing out; maybe because it represented the dismantling of our life together so that there was nothing left there to go back to, only an empty shell both physically and emotionally. But God was doing "a new thing", it was time to move on, to open my eyes, and "perceive it".

New things indeed were happening. Paul was fully in the midst of arranging his move to Australia: he now had a job, a visa, a fiancée, a place to live, and his flight was booked. And he was making plans for a wedding. This was to take place in Durham in April, so with the bride and groom in Australia it seemed as though the "home team" were going to have a lot of organising to do!

The first year in any bereavement inevitably brings the challenge of significant festivals and anniversaries where one is acutely conscious of the "absent guest". Now Christmas approached and I realised that this focal point of the year would be another challenge to us as a family as we tried to celebrate in new ways and new places. While Paul and Sara would be in Sydney celebrating in sunshine on Bondi Beach with cousins of mine, Robert, Susan, Thor, Liz, and I decided to be together at Lanehead. Gathering at 1,400 feet up in the Pennines is a challenge in itself, and the weather added its own complications as the winter snows set in. Somehow we all got there, even if Robert's car was "parked" in a snowdrift! But there was wonderful beauty in the snowy landscape, and late on Christmas Eve as I looked out of the window the snow lay deep and crisp and (not very) even, the sky was almost clear, and the moonlight illuminated a scene of total peace and beauty. On Christmas morning we walked through the snow to church.

Fortunately we had all left Lanehead by New Year's Eve when the bad weather really set in, and the dale had the worst blizzard that locals could remember for many years. In fact it snowed every day for the whole of January, and the drifts round the house reached the height of the conservatory and lingered in the drive until mid-March. The realities of living in the north-east hit home as I became snowbound in Durham City for ten days as well as being unable to reach Lanehead for six weeks.

It was New Year – 2009 was past and a new year lay open before me. It felt in some ways like a blank sheet, with an almost empty diary, which for someone used to planning eighteen months ahead and juggling episcopal and personal commitments was a major shock – no diocese, no NHS, no civic or national events. So what would 2010 hold? Life and a new journey lay before me, and one of the adjustments would be the shift to "me" rather than "us", and learning to live alone. For many who are bereaved this is one of the great challenges, and for me, as I looked back, I realised that this was the first time in my entire life when I had lived alone.

Epiphany, that post-Christmas celebration that is rather underrated but really very special, brought a familiar hymn with words that had renewed significance:

> Low at his feet lay thy burden of carefulness,
> High on his heart he will bear it for thee;
> Comfort thy sorrows and answer thy
> prayerfulness,
> Guiding thy steps as may best for thee be.[32]

These words spoke to me. Perhaps it is at times of great trauma in our lives that we become especially sensitive to the relevance and personal impact of things that otherwise pass us by. We are receptive, and God finds ways of surprising us and revealing insights of the divine in the ordinary stuff of life.

Another occasion came when watching on television the film *The Hours*, which is intriguingly constructed around the story of Virginia Woolf and her novel *Mrs Dalloway*. It ponders life and death, our choices, our self-knowledge, our masking activities, and the potential for it all to unravel. "Why does there have to be a death in the story of Mrs Dalloway?" asks Leonard Woolf, and the reply from Virginia is "because only in the face of death do we look life in the face"– only then do we come to terms with life, love it, enjoy it, and try to define happiness. As I move forward I still ponder on how I have come to look at life, and death, and mortality.

Organising a wedding was not something I had anticipated doing, but it was certainly a therapeutic distraction. Paul had chosen to be married on what would have been his father's sixty-fifth birthday – on the basis that we could either laugh or cry on that day, and the former was preferable. He planned to arrive ten days beforehand. It will be apparent by now that my life has the potential for the unexpected and unusual, and this wedding was no exception – it had the "wow" factor! It coincided with the eruption of a volcano in Iceland which totally disrupted air travel worldwide for a week, and while the bride and groom landed at Heathrow four hours before the airport shut down, Sara's parents flying separately from Perth were stuck in Dubai for six days, only arriving just two days before the wedding.

There were other unusual features: it was a two-day affair, with two services; the tiers of the wedding cake were "suitcases" for this globe-trotting couple; the best man was Paul's three-and-a-half-year-old future step-son, Charlie, supported by Paul's "best friend" Stella. And women dominated the line-up for speeches!

Paul's choice of date was a risk, but a successful compromise was reached by having a very small, private, family wedding in St John's College chapel and then the "wedding breakfast" (i.e. dinner), followed the next day by a larger and more public service of thanksgiving (outdoors, with balloons), and a proper party celebration. It became a weekend of memories, sunshine, tears, and hope for the future. In fact, three years earlier, in typical episcopal long-range diary mode, Ian and I had laid plans to celebrate this special birthday with a family house party at Parcevall Hall to follow on from our annual bishops' cell group. So, with a change of focus, and a change of venue from Wharfedale to St John's College in Durham, which had been such an important part of our lives, it felt good to have adapted and fulfilled those plans, and in a wonderful sense, Ian was very much part of the occasion.

Inevitably the wedding occupied a lot of time and effort over many weeks and months and was a very therapeutic exercise. It was in the context of leaving Peterborough, leaving the past behind, going out into a new place, making a new home, moving from regret to hope, from loss to new openings. It had been time to go; I had moved on physically from Peterborough, and gradually the family and I were moving on in other ways. We were approaching the end of an eventful year which had changed all our lives in all sorts of ways, many of them unexpected and surprising.

Time to go.
go out
go home
go away.

Reluctant or eager,
fearful or full of hope,
it's time to go.

Spirit of the way,
may we carry with us
... oil of kindness for bitter partings
... salt of courage for uphill struggle
... spice of delight for new surroundings
... water of refreshment for parched imagination
and sweet grace to surrender all we cannot
finish into other hands.

Kathy Galloway[33]

Settling Down?

How long does it take before one stops waking in the middle of the night, before a regular sleep pattern re-emerges and one stops being a devotee of BBC World Service radio programmes? How long does it take before one has any real enthusiasm for meals and for cooking again? I remembered a member of the Peterborough Cathedral congregation telling me how for the first month after her husband died she lived on cup-a-soups and ham sandwiches, and at the time I had sympathised and we had laughed, only to find myself doing something very similar when I moved to Durham and entered a new phase of my own bereavement.

Grieving is not something that can be hurried, and there is a received wisdom that it takes about two years before a bereaved person begins to feel that they have adjusted. For friends and family this is a long time and they want to feel that you are "settling down" and that you have begun to "get over it". For the bereaved it is also a long time during which the return to any sort of normality, physically, mentally, emotionally, and spiritually seems to be a painfully slow process. It is a journey on which each landmark, each significant date and anniversary, marks another step forward on the path. And I had to be conscious that my children were also walking on this path, though their experience and responses might be different.

Now we were approaching the milestone of the first anniversary of Ian's death, and somehow I felt that the emotion of the wedding weekend and of Ian's birthday had helped to release some of the tension of anticipation. The anniversary was the Friday of a bank holiday weekend, and each of us found our own individual way in which to mark it. I decided to spend the whole week at Lanehead, to be in the place that Ian had loved, to be surrounded by the many practical things that he had worked on, to browse in his library, play the piano, enjoy the view down the dale that had given him such pleasure. I found that being there on my own was not an effort – indeed it was rather a comfort – and I was able to relax and go with the flow of the week, even if the flow involved tears.

Robert decided to cycle up into the hills and sleep out in the open and remember the father with whom he had loved to walk and camp, and early in the morning he sent me a brief but poignant text message: "a night under the stars; ten minutes of cloud-free sunrise; celebrating a life." Later that day he joined me for dinner at Lanehead and we toasted Ian with another memorable bottle of claret. Paul was newly wed and back in Australia, and they went away to the wineries of the Hunter Valley to enjoy the tastings of wine, port, and cheese that Ian would have appreciated so much. Liz was in Peterborough and using the extended weekend to bond with the little kitten that she had just acquired from a Durham friend, and to share memories in familiar places. It was a special time, with special memories, for all of us – was it so small a thing, to have known and loved Ian, husband, father, brother, friend, fellow pilgrim? *Laus Deo!*

My week at Lanehead had given me time, space, quiet, a slower pace. It had not been threatening or depressing, but had gathered up a whole year of activity and distilled it into one special place. It had challenged me to look ahead, to realise that I needed to find a future, a purpose, a vision, a vocation, and to ask God: "What now?" And as we passed this anniversary, this "year's mind", almost symbolically I unpacked my jewellery for the first time since I had moved, and I wore the moss agate ring that Ian had bought for me in The Shambles in York when we were students and on a choir tour with the Ichthyan Singers and still "just good friends"!

A whole year had passed, and I looked back with amazement at all that had happened in that year. It had not been uneventful, and God had not really let the grass grow under my feet! Settling down in any conventional sense had not really happened yet. Quite apart from Ian's death and funeral, there had been: St Peter's Day; the trip to Taizé; the clearing out and packing up of The Palace; the removal and its aftermath; our fortieth wedding anniversary; the Michaelmas anniversary of Ian's ordination; visits with family to France; the practicalities of Paul emigrating to Australia leaving Liz and myself with the job of packing his boxes for shipment; Christmas; Easter; Paul and Sara's wedding; and the volcanic eruption! Oh, and a general election – the 2010 election which ended the long era of Labour government; coinciding with this first anniversary of Ian's death it took me back to his appointment as Bishop of Lewes in 1992 when that announcement was delayed because John Major was preoccupied with an upcoming general election, and the Queen was on an overseas visit. Life so often seems to be made up of such curious juxtapositions!

As I entered year two of this phase of my journey, a friend asked me if I had changed. A searching question that needed an honest answer, and as I reflected upon it I decided that my outlook on life had changed at a very basic level. It was the realisation that immortality is not an option, and that the acceptance of that changes one's perspective on life, and on death. For all of us, it is not "if" but "when". We all have to make friends with our mortality. Yet "hope springs eternal" because there is a heightened appreciation of the joys and surprises along the way, and the sense of having the God-given gift of a life to be lived, to the full, in the service of Christ.

In practical terms I entered year two deciding that if I was going to embrace life then I needed to feel brave enough to venture to plan a couple of trips on my own, first to France and then "on progress" round England to see various friends and family. In the event each of those trips would be times when I learned important lessons about myself and about the process of moving on and settling down.

First I went to St Aignan, and encountered silence again. Being there *toute seule*, alone, gave me a new experience of silence. I did not have the potential for daily contact with friends and neighbours, for morning prayer in the cathedral, Senior Common Room lunch in College, shopping in town, and all the other things that Durham offered, and in the house I did not have either radio or TV to cover the absence of voices. There was just me, the birds, the traffic, and Madame at the *boulangerie* next door. There was space, and it was not uncomfortable, but it was different.

I took myself to the local zoo (one of the best in France!), and realised that the joy of a zoo is that it slows the pace of life so that I stopped *doing* and started *observing*; I considered the art of being. Animals seem to live and move in a different time frame, no busy schedules, no plans or programmes, and it is tempting to compare the life of the social monkey, or the lethargic lamantin, with us busy humans. From another perspective I could relax and enjoy the sheer beauty, simplicity, and diversity of the created world around me, and bask in sunshine and warmth. It was time out from everyday life in Durham, time to reflect, and to think and pray more objectively, and perhaps more honestly. I was learning that, for me, there need to be spaces where I can "hear" God.

My "progress" round England took two weeks and was an enjoyable time for catching up with friends and family, but the organisation and packing up was a real effort, as was moving on from place to place, and also the problem of map-reading on my own (this being before the children decided that mother needed a Sat Nav!). I felt that I had pushed myself too far. Clearly I needed to learn to take life more slowly and more gently, and to realise that this journey really does take time and cannot be rushed; my mental, physical, and emotional energy remaining limited in a way that I was just not used to. Indeed returning to Durham at the end of the trip was an interesting experience because as I turned the corner to the house I realised that it didn't feel like coming home; it was just coming back to a place where I now lived. Belonging, and settling, both physically and socially, was going to take a lot longer.

Lanehead, however, did feel more like home, and I decided to spend much of the summer there. But it brought its own moments of revelation for me as I realised that I was struggling to cope with all that needed to be done, both in the garden and in the house, without Ian as my regular DIY expert. The determination to be "can-do" was in danger of becoming "can't-do". A summer when I had hoped to "get my act together", was in danger of falling apart. Living in two places had meant that neither was functioning properly, cleanly, tidily, etc. Gardens at both ends were running riot, odd jobs were mounting up, letters and emails kept coming, and filing was piling up and needed a proper system. When I couldn't cope any longer I would pour myself a glass of wine, enjoy the view, and sink into a good book!

And at this stage when I couldn't cope any longer, the LCF Word for the Week provided, once again, some much-needed encouragement: "I look to the hills. Where will I find help? It will come from the Lord, the Maker of heaven and earth" (Psalm 121:1–2)[34] with the accompanying comment: "Where do we look for God? Here he is seen on the hill, but in Psalm 23 he is found walking in the valley. Life must be taken as a whole with its sorrows and joys. Scenery is beautiful because the valleys are deep and the mountains are high. The valleys are part, an essential part, of the beauty of God's creation. They may be dark, cold and miserable, but taken with the mountains they make a glorious whole. As we travel the valleys of life we need to remember that Jesus promised to be with us always and look forward to being on the mountains again."[35] I knew the writer well and knew that he also had suffered a severe bereavement recently and that these words were written from the heart.

Part of the problem with not really settling down was that, for better or for worse, I was living in two houses and dividing my time between Durham and Lanehead. Both were special for me, both were important parts of my new life, and both were part of the "grand plan" that Ian and I had envisaged. I certainly did not have the energy to contemplate any major change in this arrangement in the immediate future. But putting down roots and having a sense of belonging are important, and they were taking time. I was settling but not settled, things were unpacked but not sorted, everything was in new places, which was hopelessly confusing, senior moments were par for the course. I was discovering that moving is the time when you find all those things that you had forgotten you had lost, and also the time when you lose all those things you thought you had found!

France just added another complication, but again I could not face any major decision over that house, and neither the euro nor the housing market were good news.

Finding a church and a new faith community is an important factor for a Christian when moving to a new place. But I complicated the issue by seeking to settle into not one but three churches! We had worshipped at our local church in Weardale for over twenty-five years whenever we were on holiday there, and it was a joy now to become more involved with the people there and with the whole multi-parish benefice and to get to know the current rector better. In Durham I chose to go back to the church where we had worshipped as a family during our time at Cranmer Hall, and it was good to find a mixture of familiar faces and new people, and to enter into a new relationship with that worshipping community. Cathedral life and worship were still part of the fabric of my being and so I also chose to join them there on a daily basis for morning prayer, and occasionally for evensong, and to mark the liturgical seasons with some of the special services that cathedrals do so well, and revel in the glories of cathedral music. It was, and still is, a balance that I find enriching. It is also instructive as I experience the contrast between the struggling rural church and the thriving urban church, and seek to help each to understand something of the other.

Over the years I have often gone on retreat to Benedictine communities and one of the things that has struck me about their way of life is the emphasis on stability. It is one of the vows that each person takes which will commit them to the community that they have chosen to belong to for the rest of their lives. It is both attractive and challenging for those of us whose lives involve much more change and uncertainty, and who often want to echo the words of the writer of the letter to the Hebrews (13:14) that here we have no "abiding city"! Perhaps each of us has to find our own stability as we walk our own pilgrimage path and work out our own vocation. Perhaps "being settled" has the potential for being dynamic and not just static.

But being settled, being uneventful, being predictable, were not going to be the immediate features of my life. The unexpected was, of course, about to happen again! On a memorable summer afternoon as I sat in the garden with Robert and Susan watching my little grandson Thor playing on the grass, they produced a couple of photos of ultrasound scans. This was the couple who had declared that one child was quite enough of a challenge, so it took a few moments for me to realise that they were quietly announcing the anticipated arrival of not just one, but two, more grandchildren. They were expecting twins! In Australia, Paul and Sara were already expecting a baby, so this family was growing exponentially. By the beginning of the next year I would have five grandchildren. By the beginning of the next year I would be wanting to get to know all three of the new arrivals, and this would also need to involve the challenge of a trip to Australia. My life seemed to be becoming comprised of "settling" and "moving" in equal measure!

Father, I place into your hands
the things I cannot do.
Father, I place into your hands
the things that I've been through.
Father, I place into your hands
the way that I should go,
For I know I always can trust you.

Father, I place into your hands
my friends and family.
Father, I place into your hands
the things that trouble me.
Father, I place into your hands
the person I would be.
For I know I always can trust you.[36]

Part Three

A third "determining moment". It is 12.51 p.m. on 22 February 2011. My cousin and I are kneeling at the prayer candles in the cathedral in Christchurch, New Zealand, remembering her mother in London with Alzheimers, and my Ian. Then there is a tremendous bang and jolt which shakes the whole building and she says, "We need to get out of here." We are on our feet heading for the west door when the shaking starts – floors, walls, pillars, everything in motion, and a noise of roaring and falling debris. This is a major earthquake.

Facing My Own Mortality

When I set off for Antipodean travel in January 2011 I was aware of pushing the boundaries once again, but I did not anticipate another life-changing experience. Nor did I expect to find myself the subject of newspaper headlines: "Maori prayer for quake dead; Mrs Cundy's escape" (*Church Times*); "Bishop's widow safe following amazing earthquake escape" (*Darlington & Stockton Times*); "North-east travellers caught up in the quake" (*Northern Echo*). Suddenly there was another curious blurring between the private and the public aspects of my life. So what was the sequence of ordinary events that brought me to this wholly extraordinary experience of being caught up in one of New Zealand's most devastating earthquakes? What had brought me to this near-death experience?

Plans to visit Paul and Sara in Australia had developed over the previous summer and despite the subsequent clash of dates with the anticipated arrival of the twins I had gone ahead with the bookings. I would spend a month with them in

Melbourne, and then six weeks in New Zealand reconnecting with my family's roots. The theory seemed fine, but it all felt rather daunting and I wondered how I would cope in reality. So the "safe" option had been to arrange hospitality for the most part with friends and family, breaking the long flight to Australia by staying in Singapore with a friend whom I had first met in the context of the Lawyers' Christian Fellowship, and then breaking the equally long flight home by staying in Los Angeles with an American friend whom I had met at primary school when we were only eight years old and her father was working in London.

By Christmas, my lovely granddaughter Piper had arrived in Melbourne and through the technological wonders of Skype I had been able to see her and meet her in a virtual sense. Meantime, Susan's twins had been growing apace and were clearly not going to be lightweights. In the second week of January Susan's consultant had decided that there should be an elective Caesarean at thirty-seven weeks and this was scheduled for the auspicious date of 11.1.11, which was three days before I was due to fly to Singapore. So the timetabling was tight if I was going to be available to help. In the event Robert and Susan arrived at hospital to find that there was a bureaucratic hitch because the clinic had agreed the date but not actually booked the theatre slot, and the rota for the day was full; the extra medics and midwives needed for twins were not available. The appointment was deferred for two days and a very distressed Susan returned home. By mid-afternoon, she had gone into premature labour!

The outcome was an emergency Caesarean in the evening, and Finlay and Edgar arrived safe and sound weighing in at a combined weight of over 13lb. For me, as "Granny", this was very special because those early days of their lives were something that I had been unable to share when Thor was born because at that time I was involved in caring for Ian as my priority. Likewise, it was something I had been unable to share with Piper because she was born on the other side of the world. I felt very blessed as I set off from Heathrow Airport on a trip which was, in many ways, an act of faith – another stage of moving on, a stepping out into the unknown on my own.

Family time in Australia had been very special, sharing their life, and exploring their world. I had packed the family christening dress for Piper's baptism and rejoiced to be there for the occasion, as well as to see the fourth generation wear the dress.

Then I went on to New Zealand. I had arrived there in mid-February, spending time in Wellington at the National Archives reading original letters and journals from the 1830s when my CMS forebears had arrived in the country as missionaries. Then I set off for the South Island to do the tourist thing of exploring its spectacular beauty as well as visiting friends and family. My arrival in Christchurch on Monday 21 February was prompted by a desire to see the cousin who had been one of my bridesmaids over forty years earlier, and to see Bishop Victoria Matthews whom Ian had first met in Canada over twenty years previously, and whom I had last seen at the Lambeth Conference.

I arrived in Christchurch on a lovely sunny day. My hosts' house had that lovely comfortable traditional feel – spacious and gracious – a broad window seat in the sitting room overlooking the terraced garden, a beautiful modern kitchen, a lovely Yamaha grand piano. My evening entertainment that day was to attend "Theology on Tap" – a group who met in a Christchurch pub to discuss theology over a pint and a sausage sandwich. Memorably, the speaker was the Dean of the cathedral talking about community involvement in the rebuilding after the recent earthquake the previous September, and crucial questions were raised about the long-term viability and future for the city, and the vexed question of the cost and value of preserving heritage buildings. Christchurch had been living with uncertainty and aftershocks for the last six months.

The next morning I went into town for a leisurely look round the cathedral before meeting Bishop Victoria for coffee. When I met my cousin for lunch we went back to the cathedral shop so that I could buy a children's book which seemed irresistible for my grandsons – *Grandma Joins the All Blacks*. And so it was that we had walked back through the cathedral, my cousin feeling curiously ill at ease and suggesting that we sit down quietly for a few moments at the north-west end of the nave, and then changing her mind and suggesting that we light candles over in the south aisle. Moments later, at 12.51 p.m., part of the collapsing tower came through the roof into the north-west aisle near the door by which we had entered – and the chairs where we would have sat. My till receipt for the book was timed at 12.46 p.m.

It was not until a week later that I discovered quite how tight that timing had been; quite how close we had come to death. My reaction was one of deep shock and amazement that we had walked out of the building unharmed and unaware of the immense danger we had been in and the potential alternative scenarios. Dear God, why? It is the question that we ask so often – Why? Why me? Why here? Why now? And it is followed by the question "What?" What was that about? What am I to learn? What am I to do? I had faced the mystery of mortality with Ian; now I was having to face it for myself, for real. This trip may have been an act of faith, but I had not anticipated having my faith stretched to this extent.

At the time it was the practical aftermath that concerned us. We had stumbled out of the west door into Cathedral Square in a cloud of dust so thick that one could barely see the person in front, and I heard someone say: "The tower's gone." My cousin and I found each other and had a big, dusty hug. There were a lot of dazed people and the open places were filling up as people emptied out of the buildings. The instinct was for flight, to get away from the city centre and tall buildings, so we started walking out to the suburb of Avonside where my cousin lived. It was a long walk and we passed bricks, stones, and debris strewn everywhere, traffic brought to a sudden halt, the collapsed Pyne Gould Corporation building, shattered glass, and everywhere liquefaction – that ocean of fine, grey mud oozing up through grass, pavement, and road. As we neared her home we passed the church where my cousin had been married, and saw the chancel partially collapsed, parting company with the nave, and the roof hanging precariously over both.

The house in Avonside was standing reasonably undamaged being wooden-boarded and having lost its brick chimney in the previous quake. But peering through the windows we could see that inside was chaos with even big items of furniture thrown over or moved around, and china, glass, store-cupboard food, and all loose household items strewn all over the floors. We pulled a big garden seat into the middle of the lawn and sat down together feeling the ground continue to move beneath us. We realised that we had not had lunch and were hungry, so we scavenged in the garden and picked apples, tomatoes, and lettuce. Comfort food?!

Gradually family and friends gathered and shared stories, and in this street they were all accounted for; no one was missing though some had minor injuries. Water was boiled on a primus and we shared cups of tea. Tents were erected, and in a barbecue culture there was the potential for cooking and eating outside. Everybody had their emergency "earthquake box" of essential provisions and equipment. The Dutch neighbours excelled in being calm, organised, and efficient, and their three-year-old daughter calmly talked about the "wibbly wobblys" every time there was an aftershock.

We were without water or electricity, and the telephone landline ceased to work. Some of the young went off to find distribution points for water, while others dug deep holes in the flower beds for sanitation use, i.e. very basic "pit loos"! The battery-powered radio gave some news coverage and we began to discover the full extent of the destruction, injury, and death toll. There were rumours that there were twenty-two people up the tower at the cathedral when it collapsed, one side of the Canterbury TV building had fallen away, and people were trapped in the Pyne Gould building. There were estimates of about 200 people dead, and the Central Business District was devastated. The Arts Centre where we had had a late supper after "Theology on Tap" was badly damaged and people had died in one of the shopping malls that my cousin and I had considered going to. I was acutely aware of the "might-have-beens" of life.

I realised that this would be big news worldwide and that I needed to get messages to the family. I sent the first text to Paul because it was daytime in Australia and he was likely to pick up the news first, and then sent texts to Liz and Robert who, at that time, would be asleep in England. It was also important to try and locate my hosts and see what had happened to them and to their house. Although the mobile network was rapidly becoming overwhelmed by the volume of calls I did manage to make contact, discover that they were both all right although the house was badly damaged, and agree to try and meet up the next morning. All my luggage, papers, documents, and other belongings were in that house. Well, not quite "all", because my little day-sack had got left behind in the cathedral with a random, but important, collection of personal items, including my guide book, a fleece, my book of family photos, a special small pair of binoculars, and the newly bought *Grandma Joins the All Blacks*.

The weather was not kind to us and it began to get chilly and damp so my cousin's boys found us ski jackets to keep us warm. Night fell, and it was dark with only torches to give us any light. We were all still in our day-clothes and shoes, and slept only fitfully as the aftershocks continued to come at frequent intervals. The boys were in a small tent on the lawn, my cousin and I were in a little sleep-out hut in the garden, and her husband was on the garden seat under the eaves of the hut away from the drizzle. I found that you could hear each aftershock before you felt it and in that brief interval you braced yourself and waited to see how bad it would be.

Morning brought a sense of living in limbo with the normal infrastructure and routines of life all gone. I managed to get a lift over to my hosts' house to collect my suitcase and all my belongings. I was grieved to find that their lovely home was wrecked throughout with cracks everywhere, broken windows, upturned furniture, a litter of personal treasures, and the grand piano had descended six inches through the floor. They were working out how to salvage as much as they could and then find alternative accommodation.

My next challenge was to decide what I was going to do next. People were beginning to leave town to go to friends, relatives, holiday homes, or bed and breakfast places. Without power and water, and with the inertia that comes from a general state of shock and trauma, they found it difficult to start any clear-up, and they wanted to escape from the continuous aftershocks which created tension and apprehension. As for me, I needed to salvage something from my hitherto well-organised plans. The TranzAlpine train on which I was booked was no longer running, but the travel agent in Greymouth found me a shuttle bus to take me over to the west coast and connect with the next stage of my itinerary.

So early the next morning we negotiated the damaged roads across town and the many diversions, and even found a petrol station with fuel and a working card payment system, and I reached the pick-up point for my bus. I was on my way out of Christchurch and across the Canterbury plain conscious that all the flags I passed en route were flying at half mast.

I trust in thee, O Lord, I say, "Thou art my God."
My times are in thy hand...
Let thy face shine on thy servant; save me in thy
steadfast love!

Psalm 31:14–16

For everything there is a season,
and a time for every matter under heaven:
a time to be born, and a time to die;
a time to plant, and a time to pluck up what is
planted...
a time to break down, and a time to build up;
a time to weep, and a time to laugh;
a time to mourn, and a time to dance...

Ecclesiastes 3:1–4

Alone with God, Again

For three days I had not changed my clothes, washed properly, or brushed the dust of the cathedral out of my hair. I was, in a sense, a refugee from Christchurch. But for the first time in my trip I was not going to be entertained and cosseted by friends or relatives – I was on my own, on a coach travelling down the west coast of the South Island of New Zealand, and staying in hostelries en route. I was alone.

I had found myself deeply chastened by the experience of others. There were degrees of loss in this disaster. For some it was the loss of life itself – of a family member, friend, or colleague; for others it was their home, or treasured possessions, or their job or business; and for some just the loss of their confidence, their hope for the future, the whole infrastructure of their lives. Alongside were other losses – of possessions abandoned, or a car stuck in a city car park, or a tourist holiday, or a family visit totally disrupted. And underneath, for visitors like me, is the guilt that your loss is trivial and you can move on and away, while others must live with it and its consequences. Deep down that guilt lingers, even grows. It is the guilt of the survivor.

Fox Glacier, which I reached in the late afternoon, was a wonderfully restorative experience for me. I needed to unwind somewhere where the ground didn't move. The evening was clear and warm, and I took a lovely quiet walk around nearby Lake Matheson, which is stunning in its beauty and was so peaceful. The late evening sun shone on the trees and the reflections in the still lake were magical. I could let my thoughts wander, and I could begin to talk to God and explore my deeper feelings and reactions. I had dinner at the local restaurant near the lake, and the owner of the motel where I was staying, and to whom I had talked on my arrival, kindly acted as my chauffeur. A long, hot bath, and the much-needed hair wash were the final luxuries before a long sleep. People were so kind, and I was to discover that in a curious way I had, once again, acquired both status and sympathy!

My next stop was in Queenstown with two nights in a guest house above the town, looking out at a wonderful panoramic view. I had wanted time to take a trip to Milford Sound and explore the fjords, and doing ordinary touristic things was, in a way, therapeutic and helped to restore a sense of normality. It was a weekend and on Sunday I went to the morning service in the town's Anglican church. The familiar liturgy of the Eucharist, the opportunity to be still and know the presence of God, and the sensitive preaching by the vicar, all helped to release my fragile emotions. I shed tears and once again, as at Taizé, found support and comfort from the unknown woman who was my neighbour in the pew. I found that being able to share with her and admit with honesty the depth of the trauma was an important step along the path to healing the memories. Afterwards I met the vicar who happened to be a former Bishop of Christchurch and who had been in a bible study group with Ian at the 1998 Lambeth Conference. God's world can be a small world!

For those three days after I left Christchurch I had been on my own, doing the "tourist thing" rather than visiting people. It had been three days when I had to come to terms with what had happened, cope with my emotional fragility, ask the questions and look for some answers, and interrogate the God who had, once again, delivered the totally unexpected into my life. God's timing is such a mystery, but perhaps he knew that I had needed those days and that time alone to face reality for myself and begin to work through my own reactions and responses. I had needed to learn to find my own peace with that traumatic experience, and in the event I had found some God-given space, God-given beauty, and God-given people. I had been involved again in a process of healing, but in a totally different context. Solitude is something that we often avoid, but it can be very therapeutic, and allow us to come face to face both with ourselves and with God.

By Sunday evening I was able to move on in every sense and continue my journey to friends in Dunedin. There, I was no longer alone, but instead was working through the aftermath of the earthquake in a different context. My friends had two family members staying with them who were also refugees from Christchurch and together we immersed ourselves in the news coverage, in the hope and the tragedy, hearing innumerable stories from survivors, seeing images of devastation, and realising the enormity of the recovery task ahead. It took ten days for a recovery team finally to manage to get into the badly damaged and unstable cathedral. Amazingly they did not find any bodies; contrary to speculation no one had died either in the tower or in the cathedral, which was a real miracle. Elsewhere, however, the death toll was in the region of 180 people, and many more were injured, homeless, or were just coping with damage and disruption. In a city of only 370,000 people and a country with a population of only about 4 million the ripple effect was that almost everybody knew somebody who was affected. The wider personal impact in a relatively small society was immense.

At 12.51 p.m. the following Tuesday, exactly one week after the quake, a minute's silence was observed across the whole of New Zealand. I had gone out for the day with my friends in Dunedin to the end of the Otago Peninsula, to the albatross sanctuary. We chose to go down to the beach and sit quietly there to observe our silent vigil, each of us wrapped in our own memories and our own prayers, and for much longer than a minute. The gift of silence and solitude was important and healing, and as we shared a big hug afterwards some seals came and played in the water close in to shore. We all felt that God was reminding us of the gift of life and joy.

The media caught up with me in Dunedin via the wonders of email. I knew that the organist from my church in Weardale was also in Christchurch with her husband visiting their daughter and family. What I did not know was that her close friend in Weardale, with whom she had been in touch, was married to the local journalist who had written Ian's obituary for the *Northern Echo* and would be able to put me into context. With consummate journalistic skill he had tracked me down by contacting Robert in Leeds, and so he was able to get a "first-hand report" from me for his next piece for the paper! He had an eye for the catchy emotional heading, so this one came out as "My miracle escape", and was equalled later when we had all returned to England by "Emotional reunion for quake survivors"!

It took a long time, many months in fact, for me to be able to cope with anything that shook, be it floor boards, doors banging, or other sudden noises and vibrations. So as I left the South Island and flew from Dunedin back to Wellington, I was completely unnerved by the experience of taking off into strong winds and turbulence, and even more unnerved as we came in to land at Wellington in even worse conditions. We were wrapped in cloud and the endless shaking and buffeting over which one had no control brought back all the memories. I closed my eyes, gritted my teeth, and tried not to panic! As my young neighbour sympathised, and I tried to explain to her, she told me that she had been working in a hotel in Cathedral Square at the time of the earthquake, and so we were united in the bond of common experience and shared distress.

I had journeyed a long way, in every sense, during my trip to the South Island. It had been a profound experience, part of it shared, and part of it on my own. When I finally returned home to Durham, I was again asked the question: "Have you changed?" So had I?

On reflection the answer was "yes", because I had been made even more aware of the fragility of life, of the unexpected, of the "might have been" element, and of my mortality. But at a deeper level I was even more aware of my gift of life, of God's overwhelming protection, and the need to attempt to answer the question why I had experienced another of those God-moments that makes one ask fundamental questions, and brings new direction into life's pilgrimage.

I lift my eyes to the quiet hills
In the press of a busy day
As green hills stand in a dusty land
So God is my strength and stay.

I lift my eyes to the quiet hills
To a calm that is mine to share
Secure and still in the Father's will
And kept by the Father's care.

Timothy Dudley Smith[37]

* * *

Drop thy still dews of quietness,
till all our strivings cease;
Take from our souls the strain and stress,
and let our ordered lives confess
the beauty of thy peace.

Speak through the heat of our desire
thy coolness and thy balm;
Let sense be dumb, let flesh retire;
Speak through the earthquake, wind, and fire,
O still, small voice of calm.

John Greenleaf Whittier[38]

What's It All About?

A Christmas letter from retired cousins summarised their year's activities, which were mostly focused on travel and family, by ending with the comment, "Well it all keeps us busy and happy, and that's what it's all about isn't it?" Very Epicurean! My reaction was to ask myself the question: "Well, is it?" Is that a sufficient answer to the question: "Why am I still here and not under several tons of rubble in Christchurch cathedral?"

For me, various more profound answers are found both in the Bible and in familiar liturgies – so many oft-repeated words that speak of deeper meanings and purposes in our lives.

At the end of the Communion service we pray, "Send us out into the world to live and work for your praise and glory."[39]

The prophet Micah says "What does the Lord God require of you? To act justly and to love mercy and to walk humbly with your God" (Micah 6:8, NIV).

Jesus summarises God's requirements in simple terms

"Love the Lord your God" and "Love your neighbour as yourself" (Luke 10:27, NIV).

In Psalm 71:18 we read "Forsake me not, O God, when I am old and grey-headed, till I make known your deeds to the next generation and your power to all that are to come."[40]

As a bishop's wife I attended a great many institutions of clergy to new parishes and heard the Declaration of Assent as a reminder of the faith, worship, and witness of the Church of England. Each time I had been challenged by the invitation to profess "the faith uniquely revealed in the Holy Scriptures and set forth in the Catholic Creeds, which faith the Church is called upon to proclaim afresh in each generation."[41]

Somewhere in all this I find God's calling to be faithful, to allow our lives to be a witness to that faith, to have our eyes open to the opportunities around us, and to expect that by living within the "God context" we will somehow be fulfilling his purposes for us, however unexpected the outworking of that may be.

I remember being very struck by an interview exchange that I heard on the radio with Archbishop Rowan Williams when he was being challenged about arguments for the existence of God. He replied with the simple statement that "God is not an explanation, but a context." I realised then that it does not matter whether there are highs and lows in one's spiritual life, times of doubt or when God seems absent, experiences both of the mountain tops and of the valleys, but simply that one's life has been, and is, lived in a "God context". He is the unshakeable "given" in my life, whether or not I am conscious of it – the context of my being and my faith. For me, this realisation has put those last four years into a different perspective, and opened up in a new way whatever may lie ahead.

These are not new questions and the following quotation from Hilary, the fourth-century Bishop of Poitiers, sums all this up much better than I can:

When I began to search for the meaning of life,
I was at first attracted by the pursuit of wealth
and leisure. As most people discover there is little
satisfaction in such things, and a life oriented
to the gratification of greed or killing time is
unworthy of our humanity. We have been given
life in order to achieve something worthwhile, to
make good use of our talents, for life itself points
us to eternity. How otherwise could one regard as
a gift from God this life which is painful, fraught
with anxiety, and which starts in infancy with a
blank mind and ends in the rambling conversation
of the old? It is my belief that human beings,
prompted by our very nature, have always sought
to raise our sights through the teaching and
practice of the virtues such as patience, chastity
and forgiveness, in the conviction that a good life
is secured only through good deeds and good
thoughts. Could the immortal God have given us
life with no other horizon but death? Could the

Giver of good inspire us with a sense of life only
to have it overshadowed by the fear of death?
Thus I sought to know the God and Father who
has given us this great gift of life, to whom I
felt I owed my existence, in whose service was
honour, and on whom my hopes were fixed. I was
inflamed by a passionate desire to apprehend or
know this God.[42]

My trip to New Zealand had reunited me with my roots and with some of the culture and thought patterns embedded there. The Maori have many different motifs and symbols that speak of their understanding of the world around them. One of these is "koru", and is based on the unfolding and unfurling of the fern leaf as the new growth comes each spring and takes its place in the permanence of the forest. It speaks of new beginnings, of new life, of gradual growth, of peace and harmony, and of tranquillity. For me, the journey of the last few years has been an unfolding story that speaks for itself; it has been in the daily experience of life where I have seen God at work, gently taking Ian and me forward, together and individually. All of life is a learning experience, and for us this new stage was a new experience, in all its joys and its sorrows, its highs and lows, and we found a gradual growth of faith and understanding.

This theme and concept of gradual growth and disclosure was one of the things that came out of the bible studies in Mark's Gospel that we had at Taizé. The gospel opens with the words "The beginning of the good news of

Jesus Christ" (NRSV) and proceeds with a gradual disclosure of Jesus and his mission, ministry, and teaching. This is not an immediate revelation and at several points the disciples are "blind" and their understanding has to grow slowly. Most of the parables in Mark's Gospel are about things that grow: seeds, vines, fig trees. This was an important emphasis for me as I paused to reflect and wondered if there were any instant answers. The disciples walked alongside Jesus for three years, and their understanding was still unfolding, and would continue to do so.

Being patient as we watch new growth, or experience it, is not always easy. One only really learns by experience the truth of the advice given to the bereaved that it will take time to adjust and to move on into a new life; that it is a slow process that cannot be hurried, and each stage for each individual is important. Susan Hill sums this up wonderfully in *In the Springtime of the Year*. In the book, Hill's central character struggles to come to terms with the sudden death of her husband:

> She wondered how long she would drift, and
> feel weary, in the heat of the day, and come out
> here, to sit for hours, or walk slowly between the
> trees, what would eventually break the pattern
> and waken something new in her, some desire
> or hope, and give her the energy to pursue it.
> There were times when she blamed herself and
> believed that no change could come about unless
> she herself willed it and sought after it; and times

when she knew that she could do nothing but wait, for something to come from outside and shake her alive.[43]

For me, the fern leaf has been gradually unfolding, releasing me into a new life, helping me to see a new beginning, teaching me to watch and wait, allowing me to let go of the past. But it is a continuing process, it is "work in progress".

I had travelled the world, I had survived an earthquake, I had had my horizons stretched, I had enjoyed supportive, welcoming, wonderful family and friends, I had come back to home and health and the gift of grandchildren. I had learned that journeying through this life is no "small thing"[44] – each day is a gift from God, each day is a time, an opportunity, to take risks in the service of Jesus Christ, and yet, and yet… our mortality is always there to be recognised and befriended.

Look well to this day
for it is life,
the very best of life.
In its brief course lie all
the realities and truths of existence,
the joy of growth, the splendour of action,
the power of glory.

For yesterday is but a memory,
and tomorrow is only a vision.
But today well-lived
makes every yesterday a memory of happiness
and every tomorrow a vision of hope.
Look well, therefore, to this day.

Ancient Sanskrit poem[45]

Bring us, O Lord God, at our last awakening into the
house and gate of heaven, to enter into that gate and
dwell in that house, where there shall be no darkness
nor dazzling, but one equal light; no noise nor silence,
but one equal music, no fears nor hopes, but one equal
possession; no ends nor beginnings, but one equal
eternity; in the habitations of thy glory and dominion,
world without end.

John Donne[46]

Epilogue

There were two of us on this "pilgrimage", and it seems right that the last words should go to Ian and his reflections as expressed in the sermon he preached in Peterborough Cathedral on Maundy Thursday 2008, at the service of blessing of the oils and renewal of ministerial vows.

Ian – Befriending Mortality

> He made us to be a kingdom, priests of his God
> and Father.
>
> **Revelation 1:6**[47]

I am not much given to introspection, even though the last time I used the Myers–Briggs Personality Type Indicator I emerged as "INFJ" (which was confusing as the first time I was ENTP!). But inevitably the last few months have given me more time to "be", to read, think, and pray.

As we have contemplated what it means to be a diocese inspired by God's passion, building communities which are "releasing ministry" it could have been a frustrating experience not to be able to play a full part in that process, and to have one's own vocation apparently curtailed by the frailty of the body and the debilitating effects of chemotherapy. I say "apparently" because it had reminded me that ministry – which post John Collins[48] we must understand to be about "ambassadorship" as much as "service" – is concerned with the dignity of being as well as the frenzy of spirit-filled activity.

What does it mean to be a bishop when others must take the lead, have the oversight and relieve me of those responsibilities for which I do not have the energy?

Last weekend I re-read the book that twenty-five years ago had a profound effect on my thinking about theology and ministry. Although I have not read it frequently during those years its thesis has remained imprinted on my mind. The author, Canon Bill Vanstone, begins by considering the almost universal use in the gospels and in Paul of the Greek word *paradosis* – handing over – for the act of Judas' betrayal and the change in Jesus' circumstances from that moment. Why do they use that word rather than *prodosis,* which carries the normal connotation of the English word, "betray"? Up to that point in Jesus' life he has been the active initiator, now his fate is decided by others. Both the archetypal gospels, Mark and John, make it clear in different ways that now his ministry is passive – others take the initiative – and that in that change the full significance of his "passion" is to be understood.

Vanstone asks us to consider that linguistic and theological fact alongside the increasing sense in the modern world that we are the victims, not the creative activists, subject to forces and circumstances beyond our control, and that we become the object rather than the subject of what is happening in the world. In that we become "diminished in human stature, deprived of human dignity".

But further reflection on the "handing over" of Jesus would challenge that assumption. For John, Jesus' "glory" was fully revealed in his passion when he was the patient, the object of others' decisions. We are confronted with the paradox that God who is impassible, reveals himself by being passible – allowing others to decide Jesus' fate: will they follow the crowd on Palm Sunday and become his disciples, or respond to his challenge by putting him to death? That in turn challenges our own understanding of human personality. For far from being diminished by being the patient, the object of others' choice, we become as Jesus did "figures of unique and almost unbelievable dignity". It is in waiting that we acquire our full stature – the thought that gave the book its title, *The Stature of Waiting*.[49]

We are familiar with the thought that priesthood – our priesthood as well as that of Christ – is about being as much as doing; receiving as well as giving. But if you are an activist like me, actually to be a patient – to be handed over to others for them to determine your treatment – is a salutary experience. It reminds me of my vulnerability, of that side of my humanity which is not about achievement, but about receiving the ministry of others.

Our society reveres strong and dynamic leadership; so to assert the dignity of the patient is inevitably counter-cultural. Human dignity is also about acknowledging – indeed celebrating – one's vulnerability; about receiving the ministry of the world around us as the truth of the Easter story is worked out in the re-birth of the natural world; and about receiving the ministry of one's colleagues, for whose kindness and untiring work (particularly Bishop Frank's) I am deeply grateful.

The "glory" of God is revealed this week in the human Christ, the object of others' decisions and passive acceptance of death. He never despised nor rejected his humanity, neither should we. Ministry delights in the world, rejoices that we are human, made in the image of God, whether we stride the fells of human endeavour, or wait on the decisions and the ministrations of others.

So over the last few months Canon Vanstone has been my constant companion. So has a phrase uttered by a life-long friend with whom I shared my diagnosis several months ago. "Make friends," she said, "with your mortality."

Make friends with your mortality. We all know we are mortal – destined to spend a relatively short time in this world; limited in what we can achieve while we are in our present post; curtailed as well as enriched by our humanity – but, whether we have experienced an Ignatian retreat or not, we all have to come to terms with – to befriend – it! But what does that mean?

Firstly, my own reflection has made me more aware of **the affection I have for the world**, and the passionate desire to see it reflect more fully the glory and the standards of its Creator. We live amidst incredible beauty – natural as well as human – there is beautiful scenery and there are beautiful cities and communities. We are not here to exploit it, but to act as God's stewards handing it on to the next generation in at least as good condition as we received it – a truth which our contemporaries seem at last to be taking to heart as we take seriously the effects of global warming, and the importance of the built environment for human flourishing.

One of the delights of travelling the diocese in recent years has been the re-emergence of the red kite. I rarely fail to spot one during the week – especially on the way to Corby! The red kite feeds on carrion, clearing up the mess of our destruction as we leave carcasses behind on our roads, or the remnants of other hunters' meals in the animal kingdom. That such majestic and beautiful birds should be the "dustmen" of the ornithological world perhaps gives us pause for thought about the value we invest in those whose menial and poorly rewarded tasks maintain the frailty of human living and clears up our streets and verges – our "mess".

Secondly, to make friends with our mortality, gives me **an awareness of my limitations** – a sobering yet heartening thought. I cannot possibly make the world a better place, or achieve all that I might like to, on my own. I must work with others as part of a team, both in time, and through time. Hopefully I can stand on the shoulders of others (as well as inevitably on their toes) and join hands with my colleagues in building the Kingdom of God. The temptation to omni-competence remains strong! but partnership shares the burden and both enlightens and lightens the task. "Receive the cure of souls, which is both yours and mine"[50] are not empty words; they express a deep and abiding attitude which should pervade our relationship, and your relationships with others – ordained and lay. We walk together, we work together, as you transcend my limitations and I by God's grace may occasionally transcend yours.

Jesus, as he was handed over, entrusted the task to

Peter, who denied him, to his colleagues who fled and then to a broken woman who stood weeping at his tomb!

And thirdly, it gives me what I might call the sense of **the particularity of my vocation**. Watching my former chauffeur, Guy Scott, face the difficult challenge of becoming the chaplain to the Scilly Isles (in the TV documentary *An Island Parish* on BBC Two) I was amused and heartened to hear Bishop Bill Ind admit that he could not be the parish priest of the islands. It is not his vocation! But he can use his influence and contacts with Tim Smit, the creator of Heligan and of the Eden Project, and others to help them achieve a dream of a re-built secondary school, with a speciality in environmental studies.

My mortality – the boundedness of my life – hopefully gives me the energy and the inclination to fulfil my God-given vocation and ambitions, but not to trespass into yours, except to encourage you to fulfil them. And that is something we can live with, work with, and truly befriend. That friendship does not guarantee an easy passage, but it does give me a sense of fulfilment and a deep gratitude for all that has enriched my life.

I hope the fact that this vocation is God-given, not self-made, enables me to face a new and different phase with a sense of contentment, as well as the inevitable bouts of frustration – I have to celebrate my humanity, after all! But in the end "All shall be well, and all shall be well, and all manner of thing shall be well."[51]

There must be a footnote to what I have said – indeed it is more than a footnote; it is the foundation. To find human dignity in being the object, the patient; and to befriend one's mortality can only be possible for me in a deep and transforming faith in the reality of God; the experience of resurrection and the spiritual and supportive community of the church.

Today and tomorrow we focus our minds on Jesus of Nazareth, passive and vulnerable, handed over to death, revealing in his acceptance, God's true nature as "impassible, yet passive" (*Deus non passibilis sed passus*, as Vanstone expresses it) and we are invited to release our ministry after that pattern. But on Sunday we will celebrate the "raised" Christ – again the object of other's, in this case God's, decision – for the universal testimony of the New Testament is that "God raised him from the dead".

Only in that perspective can I find myself lifted out of introspection, into a greater reality that I cannot fully understand, but which has under-girded my life and my ministry. Only in that perspective can I dare, with you, to claim a priestly vocation:

> Grace to you and peace from him who is and who
> was and who is to come… and from Jesus Christ,
> the faithful witness, the firstborn of the dead, and
> the ruler of the kings of the earth.
>
> To him who loves us and freed us from our
> sins by his blood, and made us to be a kingdom,
> priests serving his God and Father, to him be glory
> and dominion forever and ever. Amen.
>
> **Revelation 1:4–6,** NRSV

Postscript

In March 2013 the congregation in Canterbury Cathedral and television viewers worldwide saw Justin Welby enthroned as the 105th Archbishop of Canterbury, wearing the "Cundy" cope and mitre. This beautiful set of vestments was made and embroidered by Juliet Hemingray[52] and was the wonderfully generous gift to Ian from Cranmer Hall and St John's College when he left Durham in 1992 to become Bishop of Lewes in Sussex. When Ian died his coffin at the funeral was draped with the cope and the mitre placed on top, and so they had very special associations for me and also for the family, and we retained them in the hope that one day this "mantle" would pass to the right person.

When Justin was appointed as Bishop of Durham it seemed like the perfect answer – he had been a student at Cranmer Hall during our last three years there; both families had worshipped at the same church and become good friends. Ian had appreciated Justin's many talents and we had been present at his installation as Dean of Liverpool shortly after the diagnosis of Ian's cancer. So the offer was made and the robes fitted perfectly, and when, in November 2011, Justin wore the cope and mitre for his enthronement in Durham Cathedral it seemed that they had "come home" to Durham. Ian would have been delighted, but he would have been amazed when, in little more than a year, Justin moved to Canterbury and the "Cundy" cope and mitre moved with him and have become one of the iconic images associated with the new archbishop!

We may have "let go" of Ian but his legacy lives on, not just in the tangible form of the cope and mitre, but in the lives of the many people, like Justin, whom he encountered, taught, and influenced.

Laus Deo!

Acknowledgments

There are always people without whom "things would not have happened", and among the many such in my life I want to record my thanks here to the following:

To my children, Robert, Paul and Elizabeth, whose story this is as well, and my grandchildren who will sadly never know their grandfather but who bring ongoing joy and hope for the future.

To Grace Sheppard and Ruth Etchells who first gave me confidence to write but did not live to see the fruits of their encouragement.

To Caroline Chartres for opening up the world of publishing to me.

To David Wilkinson, at St John's College, Durham, who has continued to give me confidence, and to mentor and advise me.

To Frank White, our suffragan bishop, and his wife Alison, who travelled with us on this road, together with the rest of the senior staff at Peterborough.

To Terry Burley our wonderful GP, and to Jeremy Steele and the medics at Barts Hospital, without whom Ian could not have continued to live life to the full and "keep the show on the road".

To the people and clergy of the diocese of Peterborough, and to our many "travelling companions", for their constant love, support, and prayers.

To the churches and congregations who support me now at St John's, Neville's Cross, and St Thomas, Heatherycleugh.

To Justin Welby for writing the foreword and for being an ongoing part of this story.

To those who patiently read earlier drafts and gave me their very honest and creative comments, especially Ruth Etchells, Deborah Barff, and Judy Turner, and to my brother-in-law, David Cundy, for his detailed proof-reading and comments.

To Tony Collins, Jenny Ward, and the team at Monarch for their editorial skills and for guiding a novice writer through the complexities of commercial publishing.

Notes

1. R. S. Thomas, from "Pilgrimages" in *Later Poems 1972–1982*, Papermac, 1984, p. 125.

2. Extract from John O'Donohue, "For the Traveller" in *Benedictus: A Book of Blessings*, Bantam Press, 2007, p. 70.

3. From John O'Donohue, "For the Traveller" in *Benedictus: A Book of Blessings*, Bantam Press, 2007, pp. 69–70.

4. Francis Jeune, Bishop of Peterborough (1864–68).

5. Michael Hawthorne, adapted from his "Word for the Week" for the Lawyers' Christian Fellowship, 3 September 2007. Habakkuk 2:1, 3 is adapted from the NKJV.

6. R. S. Thomas, "Kneeling", from *Selected Poems 1946–1968*, Bloodaxe, 1986.

7. Ian Miller, adapted from his "Word for the Week" for the Lawyers' Christian Fellowship, 11 November 2007. Quote from Hebrews is NIV.

8. John Bell and Graham Maule, The Wild Goose Resource Group, Iona Community, Glasgow.

9. Dag Hammarskjöld, from *Markings* (his collected journal entries), 1964.

10. "Lord Jesus, Think on Me", by Synesius of Cyrene (375–430), translated by Allen W. Chatfield (1808–96).

11. John O'Donohue, "For the Interim Time" in *Benedictus*, Bantam Press, 2007, pp. 134–35.

12. Hymn by Johnson Oatman, 1897.

13. Hymn by William Cowper (1731–1800).

14. Originally a Rodgers and Hammerstein song from the 1945 musical *Carousel*, but since popularised on football terraces.

15. *Common Worship: Services and Prayers for the Church of England*, Church House Publishing, 2000.

16. Taken from The Book of Common Prayer.

17. Brian McAvoy, in Peterborough Diocesan Cycle of Prayer, Autumn 2008.

18. "Praying our goodbyes", from Church Mission Society's *Prayerlines*, May 2009.

19. From "O Jesus, I Have Promised", John Ernest Bode (1816–74).

20. Christian Prayers, 1578.

21. John Bunyan, *Pilgrim's Progress* – the death of Mr Valiant-for-Truth.

22. Jamie Harrison, St John's College SCR President, 2007–2012.

23. Traditional Celtic Blessing.

24. In 970 Dunstan of Canterbury and Oswald of York were in Peterborough for the consecration of the second abbey in the presence of King Edgar.

25. Extract from *The Book of a Thousand Prayers*, compiled by Angela Ashwin, Zondervan, 2002, p. 247.

26. Aria from *Orpheus and Eurydice*, 1762 opera by Gluck.

27. *Common Worship: Services and Prayers for the Church of England*, Church House Publishing, 2000.

28. *A Year with Dietrich Bonhoeffer: Daily Meditations from His Letters, Writings, and Sermons* (Carla Barnhill, ed.), HarperCollins, 2005, p. 49.

29. Taizé Community chant.

30. Taizé Community chant.

31. Matthew Arnold (1822–88), from the "Hymn of Empedocles".

32. John Samuel Bewley Monsell, 1863.

33. Kathy Galloway, adapted from "Time to go", from *Talking to the Bones*, Triangle, 1996.

34. This precis of Psalm 121 appears in a window in Hatfield Parish Church.

35. John Head, adapted from his "Word for the Week" for the Lawyers' Christian Fellowship, 4 July 2010.

36. Jenny Hewer, "Father, I Place into Your Hands", Kingsway Thankyou Music, 1975.

37. Timothy Dudley Smith, Hope Publishing Company, 1973.

38. John Greenleaf Whittier, Quaker poet (1807–92).

39. Taken from *Common Worship: Services and Prayers for the Church of England*, Church House Publishing, 2000.

40. *Common Worship: Services and Prayers for the Church of England*, Church House Publishing, 2000.

41. *Common Worship: Services and Prayers for the Church of England*, Church House Publishing, 2000.

42. Hilary, Bishop of Poitiers (315–67), from the treatise "On the Trinity".

43. Susan Hill, *In the Springtime of the Year*, Vintage, 2012, p. 208.

44. Matthew Arnold; see note 31, above.

45. Kalidasa, fourth-century Sanskrit poet and dramatist.

46. John Donne (1572–1631), from a sermon preached in 1627 and adapted by Eric Milner White, who omitted some phrases, for example, "no foes nor friends, but an equal communion and identity".

47. Adapted from the NIV of Revelation 1:6.

48. See the research and work on the nature of Christian ministry by John N. Collins in *Diakonia: Re-interpreting the Ancient Sources*, Oxford University Press, 1990.

49. W. H. Vanstone, *The Stature of Waiting*, Darton Longman and Todd, 1982.

50. These are the words used in the Service of Institution or Licensing of a new incumbent in a pastoral ministry as the bishop hands the licence to the priest.

51. Julian of Norwich (1342–1416), from *Revelations of Divine Love*.

52. Juliet Hemingray, Church Textiles, Derby, www.church.textiles.co.uk

Picture credits

Cover photograph by Peter Moyse, Helpston, Peterborough

Picture section p. 1: portrait by Ben Davies-Jenkins, www.bendjart.co.uk

Picture section p. 7: top photo by David Collins, Oxford, www.davidcollinsphotography.co.uk

Background to picture section features Cundy cope and mitre, designed by Juliet Hemingray and photographed by Tim Heeley.

All other images courtesy of the author.

Text credits

Extracts pp. 21, 61 from *Benedictus* by John O'Donohue © John O'Donohue, published by Bantam. Reprinted by permission of The Random House Group Limited.

Extract p. 52 taken from 'Enemy of Apathy' (Wild Goose Publications, 1988). Words John L. Bell & Graham Maule, copyright © 1988 WGRG, Iona Community, Glasgow G2 3DH, Scotland. Reproduced by permission. www.wgrg.co.uk

Extract p. 114 from *Saying Goodbye* © Ruth Burgess (2013) Wild Goose Publications, Glasgow. Reproduced by permission.

Extract p. 117 from *Letters and Papers from Prison, The Enlarged Edition* by Dietrich Bonhoeffer, SCM Press 1971 © SCM Press. Used by permission of Hymns Ancient & Modern Ltd.

Extracts p. 125 from "Jesus le Christ" and "See I am Near" © Taizé Community. Used by permission.

Extract p. 146 from the song "Father I Place Into Your Hands" by Jenny Hewer, copyright © 1975 Thankyou Music. Adm. by Capitol CMP Publishing worldwide excl. UK & Europe, admin by Integritymusic.com, a division of David Cook songs@integritymusic.com. Used by permission.

Extract p. 165 from "I Lift My Eyes" by Timothy Dudley-Smith (b.1926) © Timothy Dudley-Smith in Europe and Africa. © Hope Publishing Company in the United States of America and the rest of the world. Reproduced by permission of Oxford University Press. All rights reserved.

Extract pp. 170-171 from *In the Springtime of the Year* by Susan Hill, published by Vintage. Reprinted by permission of The Random House Group Limited.